LAUNCH YOUR LIFE

Creating a Life in Service of God

LAUNCH YOUR LIFE

Creating a Life in Service of God

Philip E. and Elizabeth J. Bruns

Carpenter's Son Publishing

Launch Your Life

Published by Carpenter's Son Publishing, Franklin, Tennessee

Published in association with Larry Carpenter of Christian Book Services, LLC
www.christianbookservices.com

Cover Design by Carrie Bruns

Interior Design by Suzanne Lawing

Edited by Robert Irvin

Editorial Assistance by Michelle Diekmeyer

Printed in the United States of America

978-1-949572-39-1

To Elise, Carrie, Allison, and Rose:
you are more inspiring to us than you know.
PEACER!

Contents

I-P-A: What Is That?

What one does is what counts, not what one had the intention of doing.

– Pablo Picasso[1]

A few years ago, we discussed traveling to Europe at some time in the future. In that conversation, we expressed the same desire as one another, going so far as to lay out our thoughts on our five favorite cities and countries. London, Germany, Switzerland, Italy, and Scandinavian countries were all on our list—along with some other contenders. But we landed on a trip to Paris as our top choice, the beautiful City of Lights. Thoughts of making the trip, climbing the steps of the Eiffel Tower, gazing upon the Mona Lisa, walking the Champs Élysées to the Arc de Triomphe, and strolling the gardens of the Palace of Versailles were enough to bring a bit of wonder to our thoughts and dream that it could come true. It would be a goal for some years ahead, we knew, but we had our intentions firmly in place.

After a couple of years, we revisited the thought of planning the trip, starting with seeking a definitive answer to this question: could we make this trip a reality? Perhaps in the months that had passed since we first discussed the possibility, our thoughts had moved from "if" questions to the more practical "how." We both wanted to make the vacation happen, but there had been other matters that had developed that we would need to consider in our planning. These were mostly financial and timing issues, so we needed to decide if we thought this would be money and time well spent. Additional concerns on the length of time and scope of activities also needed discussing. But we launched into the task. We began planning with excitement!

There are dozens of fantastic museums, palaces, and old cathedrals to see in the Paris metropolitan area. So, finding a place to stay that is within easy proximity to the rails that would allow access to the surrounding area was imperative; walking and rail would be our two modes of transportation while there. After much online searching and recommendations from a Parisian who is a friend, we found a quaint one-bedroom apartment on the third floor of a building nestled in the heart of Paris. It was walking distance to some sites, but more importantly, an easy stroll to two separate rail stations. The flights and other travel details were also researched, then chosen. But the pinnacle moment came when the planning turned into action and a credit card was used to pay for the flight and apartment reservations!

Later, we packed and made our way to the airport. We were going to Paris.

Picasso was right. We had the best of intentions, and we talked about them in detail. But without the planning, the intentions would have just been passing thoughts. Further, without the action, the intentions and the planning would have remained much-deliberated dreams, and we never would have needed to pack our bags. If you want to Launch Your Life, you need all three: Intention, Planning, and Action—or, *I-P-A*. If you are legal to drink and enjoy an occasional beer, you may be familiar with those three letters: I-P-A. But our I-P-A, *this I-P-A*—Intention, Planning, and Action—will provide you with many more life opportunities and benefits than an India Pale Ale.

While writing this book, we found several thoughts that touched our hearts in ways that challenged us in faith, action, and character. In the same way, we expect that you will find opportunities for growth in your character, spirituality, or life in general. Keep the thought of *I-P-A* at the forefront of your mind. Do you want to find a new college major or a new job? *I-P-A*. Would you like to enhance your career development or consider additional education? *I-P-A*. Have a desire to learn more about God's Word? *I-P-A*. Do you want to grow closer to God or a friend? *I-P-A*. Want to go to Paris? *I-P-A*.

This book will help you directly with the I and the P, and we hope it will inspire you on the A, but the follow-through ultimately will be up to you. Heed Picasso's words as you read. We want you to hear the call to faithfully move forward in life and feel empowered to do so. Imprint *I-P-A* on your heart, engrain it in your mind, and make it part of your soul. And where one door shuts, keep moving forward and looking for another that opens.

If "plan A" in your action plan doesn't go as hoped, remember there are twenty-five more letters in the alphabet—and more than three thousand characters if you're in China!

This book is not about your future. It is one *for* your future. So let's make it count.

IF PETER CAN CHANGE . . .

Then Peter stood up with the Eleven, raised his voice and addressed the crowd: "Fellow Jews and all of you who live in Jerusalem, let me explain this to you; listen carefully to what I say" (Acts 2:14).

It was a moment Peter would never forget. The insights and unshakable faith that Jesus gave him when they walked together were ready to be unleashed through Peter's voice. Jesus was gone. The fresh memories of Jesus' life, crucifixion, and resurrection had to be at the forefront of Peter's mind as Jesus' ascension had taken place only a few weeks before. Consumed by the Holy Spirit, Peter and his peers began to share the good news of Jesus and the power of the resurrection. Before Peter were thousands of souls, many of whom had traveled a long journey from their home to be in Jerusalem. Men and women watched and intently listened as Peter called them to do.

The crowd was vast. It had to be an eye-opening moment for Peter and the people as they would collectively understand the connection between their sins and Jesus' death. And through Peter's words they would turn and become followers—disciples—of Jesus, an astounding thing to consider. Peter must have thought back to the day he was on a boat and Jesus shouted to him to throw his nets to the other side. That action turned a fish-less night into a night so full of fish that the nets began to burst. Peter saw this kind of thing again and again with his Lord. But now, while Jesus' presence was felt in Spirit instead of the flesh, he was still seeing marvelous things happen. And Peter was beginning to see how he would impact the world.

There was little chance Peter pictured himself in this position years earlier. The loudmouthed fisherman had grown substantially since the beginning. His heart and character had changed since he dropped his nets to follow Jesus. He wasn't known as a leader, for it was later written in Acts that Peter and some of the others were just unschooled, ordinary men (4:13). After all, he was a simple fisherman. The gospel paints a picture of his flawed character, one that was rash, quick in judgment, irrationally emotional. And on the positive side of his character, he was willing to help others, take a stand, and surrender to God's will for his life. And through this journey with Jesus, Peter saw that miracles could happen.

At some point in his time with Jesus, he resolved to use his whole life, including his dreams, for Jesus' more significant cause. He resolved to be a fisher of men.

We assume you have already read about Peter in God's Word, so as you begin this book, consider the incredible conversion you see in his life. He started as a man throwing nets into quiet waters with a few others, just a regular guy at work. He *became* a faithful disciple who thousands would look to for guidance and a plan of salvation. The Spirit, combined with Peter's words, moved the hearts of the thousands who listened on that one particular day to respond and be baptized (Act 2:40-47). Amazingly, the transformation did not end there, or even in his lifetime. Far beyond what Peter would have thought at the time, his words are still read two thousand years after being spoken, and they continue to change lives for those who listen to them. Today, millions read his words, see hope in the gospel, and realize what God can do through one soul.

But how did God take Peter and change him into a compelling, bold speaker? What did God do to grow him from a dime-a-dozen fisherman into a one-of-a-kind fisher of men? We see in the gospel how God guided his dreams, his gifts, and his temperament. We can also see how God used difficulties and challenges to guide and focus his dreaming. Finally, we can see what *didn't* happen. Peter didn't just wake up one day and—*poof!*—he was the leader, preacher, and teacher we see in Acts 2. Peter's desire and dreaming qualities were combined with a willingness to learn. He surrendered himself to be the leader that Jesus called him to be, allowing him to change and grow.

Maybe another way to think about this is to consider how God blessed Peter and planned for this life long before it was visible. He was knit together in his mother's womb for this exact moment. The raw material was there, but it had not been developed or sharpened before his time with Jesus. In his sinful ways, he neither recognized his gifts nor realized how to use them for God's higher calling. He likely hadn't spent time dreaming about what he could do for God before he met Jesus. But Peter had a soft heart for God's will as he walked with Jesus and as Jesus taught him. He had a heart that God would use for His purposes. Jesus showed him what it meant to fish for men, to be a disciple of his Lord, and then honed his talents and gifts for the future.

Without choosing Jesus and discipleship, Peter would have amounted to nothing but a nameless, impetuous fisherman. We would not know him today.

Peter's story is an incredible one—it is characterized by transformation and growth. He grew from an insignificant, ordinary guy to a world-changer. It is doubtful he would have seen anything like this coming in his youth.

Believe it or not, in a similar way, you have a chance to participate in the incredible story of *you*. Your account will be unique and can also be a story of unimaginable impact and faith. Are you ready to open your eyes?

You have more similarities to Peter than you probably think. Peter learned to tie knots to prepare a net for his job. Perhaps you are a budding designer, plumber, or engineer. Maybe you're a budding you're-not-sure-what! Peter had hopeless nights where his work didn't go well. You have had tough times in school or at work as well. He learned how challenging it is to keep his eyes on Jesus; you've struggled to persevere in your faith. He had successes and failures. You've had them too. Peter gained inspiration from how special it was to be chosen by

God; you can see how God has touched your life, and you are likely encouraged by this as well. Like Peter, you have talents, experiences, and dreams. While Peter's story lives in history, God is shaping you for a remarkable future.

We believe that if you are faithful to God, God has a plan for you to impact this world for Him. And we think it is an impact more substantial than you realize, and certainly more extensive than what the enemy tells you or wants you to believe. You're not insignificant to God, and He has a plan!

Peter's life is one example of many from which we can draw inspiration. It's not hard to find other examples in God's Word. And God doesn't just give us men. In later chapters, we will look at both biblical men and women and see how God used them, their talents, their careers, and their characters in surprising ways for His cause. You will see how their characters and their skill sets were a blessing in the world at their time. Just as God has chosen you, you will see how God wanted them for higher purposes than they ever imagined. And we'll discuss how God has prepared you for great dreams where you can use your skills as a blessing to the world.

You will read about how to approach a career, make career choices, and how careers can work, but more importantly, how God values you, even in your secular job. We believe God has provided other inspiration, and we will explore other modern-day stories as well. Hopefully, you'll be moved in new ways and encouraged by a God who loves you desperately. Through these stories, and with the help of practical advice, we hope to stir your heart to bold action.

Finally, we hope and pray this book will inspire you to greater heights than you thought possible in service to God. We hope it will shine a huge light on what a fantastic person you are, and that you will see even more, how important you and your talents are to God and His mission to seek and save the lost.

We hope it will encourage you to be eternally grateful for God and faithful to Him as you grow, and that you will never give up on Him.

PART I

It Starts with God

Chapter One

DARE TO SOAR

Do you not know? Have you not heard? The Lord is the everlasting God, the Creator of the ends of the earth. He will not grow tired or weary, and his understanding no one can fathom. He gives strength to the weary and increases the power of the weak. Even youths grow tired and weary, and young men stumble and fall; but those who hope in the Lord will renew their strength. They will soar on wings like eagles; they will run and not grow weary, they will walk and not be faint (Isaiah 40:28-31).

This Isaiah passage is a favorite of many faithful men and women today. It's a Scripture that speaks of God's eternal presence and His unwavering power, and it carries a grace-filled promise for us. These are inspirational words about dreaming in Him. They also call us to go to God, to lean on Him, and to allow Him to change us into people who impact the world. In pursuing God we have hope, and, specifically, hope to dream. In fact, because of Christ, we should be less afraid to dream. We should expect Him to use us and we should desire for Him to do things with our lives that only He can do.

In the introduction, we briefly discussed the transition in Peter's life. Now consider the change in his dreams and goals. Early in his life, before what we read about him in God's Word, what would have been the focal point of Peter's dreams? Did he have hopes for his life? If he did, they most likely changed to a much higher calling anchored in God's grace and for God's purposes. Among many others, we find Jesus calling Peter and the other disciples to go to "all nations" (Matthew 28:18-20), substantially farther than they ever thought to travel before. And just as when Jesus first called him, we see again in John 21:15-23 that his Lord looked Peter in the eyes and personally called him to "follow me!" Both moments came near the end of Jesus' time here on earth, and both were a call to dream, be faithful, and have a life of impact for God's glory.

We'll come back to Isaiah's amazing text further, as well as provide other inspiration in God's Word. But there are contemporary stories of significant accomplishments to consider as well. Let's pause for a moment and look at what it takes for dreams to come true. Let's explore a story of two dreamers from recent history—their efforts and their achievements.

It is a story of two brothers, both early in their careers, who stood on the eastern shore of the United States in the early years of the twentieth century. They had been working on their dream for a few years. For starters, they were consumed with an exhaustive study of birds. Libraries and other resources had been a help to them, but on this day, they watched several species of birds flying around the ocean's edge.[2] A flicker. A pelican. But mostly gulls glided in the stiff ocean breeze or walked on the sandy shore in front of these brothers. They were watching these birds closely, but they were also illustrating them and their corresponding movements.

Because they spent significant time at the ocean's edge over a few years, the brothers built a small shop along the shoreline, a safe distance from the water's edge, but in the middle of their "dream space," which was among the birds. At the shoreline they lived, slept, and worked their dream. With their location on the beach, sand found its way into their workshop and rain leaked through the roof during coastal storms—but still, this space was enough for them. Sometimes one brother would be in the shop, the other outside, or many times they were working together either watching the birds in the sun or inside the shop doing their work. To the casual observer, they always seemed to be busy doing . . . something.

Periodically, the locals would stroll by and hear or see them at work. Mostly, they observed the men talking, sketching, or engaged in woodworking, all in service of some sort of project happening inside the shop. Their intention was not to be secretive about their work and dreams, but most locals had no idea what they were doing. They just found the men curious; at times, just plain entertaining.

One day, the stiff breeze gusted inland while the clouds floated overhead against the blue skies. A few coastal residents happened upon the two men. Once again, the two men were observing the birds intently. Although the men were a reasonable distance away, their strange movements caught the residents' attention in a different way. The taller one had a notebook out and was sketching and writing as he pleased. The other man was seen humorously flapping his arms and hands as if he were a bird! Some thought he was foolishly playing; others felt the pair were just odd. A few snickered. Suddenly, the taller one set his notebook aside and, together, both men engaged in the arm-flapping, hand-waving game, causing more chuckling and even starting rumors. After watching for a few minutes, the locals just shook their heads and went on their way.

The townspeople didn't know or understand the details or purpose of what the two men were doing, and, for the most part, they didn't care. They were blind toward their work and critical of them. In time, though, they continued to observe the men and their persistence, their trial and error, and the determination regarding their work. As still more time passed, it became clear they weren't acting like birds on the beach for mere entertainment; these men were trying to emulate the birds' movement. They were sketching details and illustrations of the birds and their wings and applying what they learned on their project inside the building.

The men were not playing after all. They were dreaming about doing something never done before, about going places never previously explored. They were dreaming of flying. They were brothers from Ohio, Orville and Wilbur Wright. After a few years of research on the Kitty Hawk, North Carolina shore, including many failures as they trekked their path toward success, the brothers would create the first controlled flight of a machine. Air travel was born.

The amount of effort and clear, focused dreaming can't be overstated. The success of their dream took consuming work over many years. They needed support and help from a few others, including their sister Katherine, who stayed home in Dayton to manage the Wright family affairs. She was a stronghold for the brothers for many years. And while the Wright brothers are better known, Katherine was invaluable to the team for years. Her contributions to their efforts were no less important than Orville's or Wilbur's. In a unique role while the brothers labored in Kitty Hawk, Katherine nearly single-handedly ran the family bicycle shop back in Ohio while serving as a conduit of information for the brothers to their father and the local press, among others. Both a college graduate and a school teacher, she would become one of the first woman ever to fly.[3] In the years following the first successful flights, Katherine gained notoriety as she often accompanied her famous brothers in their travels throughout Europe and America. Big dreams often require teams or families or churches to make them concrete, to turn them into reality.

Other visionary people had the same dream: to fly a controlled machine that could carry a man or woman. Four hundred years ahead of the Wrights, Leonardo Da Vinci created machine designs in hopes of flying, but he never saw success. In the years leading up to the notable day of the first successful flight in Kitty Hawk—December 17, 2003—there were others who made attempts to fly. In most cases, however, their efforts came crashing to the ground—often literally, sometimes ending their lives.

WHY THEY WERE DIFFERENT

What was the difference? Why did the Wright siblings attain success where many others failed? Was their dreaming that much better? There are several reasons why fortune fell their way, but mostly it can be credited to their study of birds and its application to their flying machine. And despite the Wright brothers not being a story of faith that we read in God's Word, there are numerous principles here we can take to heart. We know it took much study and preparation, as well as perseverance, to overcome the unknowns and failures. Before their time in Kitty Hawk, the brothers spent months reading and studying about birds. They would sketch and make numerous diagrams.

It also took a bold, non-traditional vision. There were no books to study on flying machines or airplanes, no information on the mechanics of wings or the effects of air pressure on an aircraft. The brothers were envisioning what no one else could. The Kitty Hawk locals had enjoyed those same birds for many years, but only for entertainment. The Wrights saw a vision. They observed the birds with a desire to learn and create something that would leave an impact on this world. They dared to act on that dream. This vision led to deliberate efforts in each of their roles to make plans, communicate, and work efficiently. The brothers were willing to face the dangers, the difficulties, and the rough days. They also determined to keep after their goals and dreams when failure struck. They worked long hours crafting each part for the plane, and when those failed, they made new ones. They continued to persevere—more and more toward that splendid day when they would make their first flight.

It's easy to read about the dreams of others, to do so simply to find a good story or an interesting read. We can sing songs about dreaming or listen to Dr. King speak his majestic words in the famous "I Have a Dream" speech. But it's an entirely different matter to make things personal and go beyond being a dream spectator to participating in *your own* intentional work of realizing a dream.

God wants us to make things personal. He believes in us and wants us to dream. And while the Wright brothers' accomplishments are amazing, and historical, there is no more enduring inspiration than a dream that comes from God. The passage in Isaiah 40 that we first read is about dreaming. "Those who hope in the Lord will renew their strength"; "they will soar on wings like eagles"; "they will run and not grow weary, they will walk and not be faint." These are all inspirational words about dreaming. They inspire us to strive to make possible what we think is impossible. The challenge is to open our eyes to things not seen. They are God's words that give us hope of an extraordinary future and endless possibilities. But as it was with the Wrights, victorious dreaming takes passionate effort on our part. We need focused ambition and the ability to make deliberate decisions to realize a great dream. And, just like the Wrights, we will need to learn to overcome setbacks. It's not always easy, but God is there to provide the path.

ONLY YOU CAN DREAM FOR YOU

As you launch into the early part of adulthood or the next stage of your life, think about your future. Where can God take you and what impact can you make that can only come from you? Where will you be in one year? Five years? We advise you to focus on dreaming in the one- to five-year horizon. Because there are so many variables in life, it is very difficult to think about time much further than five years into the future. The important thing is to realize that it begins with you; no one else can dream for you. For sure, you may have a loving parent, a close sibling, a friend, or a spouse who has high hopes for your future. And yet even if the whole world has high expectations for your life, your future comes down to you and your thoughts and choices for your life. God chose Peter, but Peter also chose God and decided to follow Jesus.

Only you can dream for your future and put great intentions and then planning and action in place to allow God to do astonishing things through you. Perhaps you are in your last years of college, or maybe you've finished and you're ready to move on. If you are already working in your career, perhaps you've found your dream job. Or possibly, like so many others at the beginning of their careers, you're not on a path that is entirely working for you. Regardless of where you are on your journey, we've written this book to help you dream, plan, and act toward that dream now. And just as the Wrights had to assemble their plane to achieve their goal, this book is intended to help you gather the parts of your aircraft and discern the specifics needed to help you meet yours. We're written this book to help you see and define a dream, plan through a transition to act on your vision, and inspire you to launch to a phenomenal time ahead, enabling God to use your unique gifts for Him.

THE VALUE OF TEAMS

Dreaming is infectious! Like a stone plopping into calm water, clear inspiration from God for yourself, combined with hope in the Lord (Isaiah 40), will produce a ripple effect for those around you. Working our dreams into the context of groups can provide additional dynamics to examine and inspire. Nothing is more fun than spending time with a group on a joint mission, and many times, dreaming as a group or team project produces something better than would emerge from an individual. For example, if you're working on a group project in class, your desire to do well on the project will unquestionably help the group toward that end, especially if your underlying goal is to glorify God. If you are employed, you probably work with others, and your group will have goals or a specific project you are working on concurrently. If you are dreaming in a small group in your church, it shows in your spirit and actions, whether you're the leader or not, because the effect on your group will be aspirational. The key is to dream and dream in a way that creates intention and forward progress toward the goal.

The effect of the Wrights' success was enormous. It led many others to fly, and within a short few years this newly created industry blossomed into transatlantic flights and new generations of people dreaming of flying higher and faster. It all started with two visionary men who took notes in a tattered journal and studied birds on a deserted beach in North Carolina. But that is just flying! Consider

Jesus as a dreamer, hopeful of the future while He walked the earth. He chose twelve men, including the fisherman Peter, and dreamed for these individuals. He had visions for what they would do—even greater things than He had done. He helped them grow from living by what they see to living by the unseen and becoming dreamers for God. Over time, others would be inspired to follow. His disciples increased in numbers because of the hope that Jesus gave and the forgiveness only found in Him. Jesus taught, shared, and loved many. And in Jesus' final days, He gave a vision to His disciples to take His words to the world. Shortly after that, Peter stood in front of the crowds in Acts 2 and called them to listen to him. The impact was profound.

Let's again consider Katherine Wright and her role in the Wrights' pursuit. While not known as well as her brothers (after all, everyone knows them as the Wright *brothers*), her role was critical to their success, and it was a role she happily accepted. Sometimes it isn't always obvious what part you play in the dreams God has for you, or you don't see your value in a group, especially if you are not in the leading role. However, that does not make you any less valuable. Consider the early disciples who listened to Peter on the day he stood up to speak to the crowd. We do not know the names of most of the men and women present, but to God they were no less important or any less a part of the story. They just played a different role in that incredible, magical time. Dreaming for God, ultimately, is done in service of His dreams for the people He created, and we should be receptive to the part we play in God's dreams for our lives and fully trust Him along the way. Regardless of your role, be a dreamer! Ephesians 2:10 says, "For we are God's handiwork, created in Christ Jesus to do good works, which God prepared in advance for us to do." You are essential in your role with the exact gifts you possess.

Because the phrase "dreaming for God" can be a bit vague, especially with what seems like a long future ahead, it's important to discuss *productive* dreaming and how it should show up in our day-to-day living. The truth is dreaming should touch every area of your life, and our dreams should drive us day to day in our spirit and what we choose to do. We want you to recognize the gifts you have received from God, including your talents, experiences, and spiritual gifts and give them entirely to Him for His use. This surrendering to God should inform your college choice, your employment, your relationships, and more.

If you love God, you should dream that He uses your life in a way that fits with His will. The creator of all that we see wants to use you! This fact is simply incredible when we can see and believe this. In response to God's love for him, Peter lived this example. His role was unique to Peter, just as God has a position unique for *you*.

GOD DOESN'T DO ORDINARY

Like so many things, when God is involved, amazing things can happen. What Bible story is ordinary? Regular boat trips became sea squalls that soon after are immediately calmed (Luke 8:22-25). Fishing trips turned into walking on water (Matthew 14:22-36). Waterlogged wood turned into an engulfing fire (1 Kings 18:16-38). People stuck between the sea and a pursuing army walked through water on dry land to escape (Exodus 14). Three young men huddled together with a mysterious fourth person in a fiery furnace and walk out unscathed (Daniel 3). And somehow, a couple of fish and some bread was enough to feed thousands (Matthew 14:13-21). God doesn't do mediocrity. When He is involved, amazing things happen.

But it takes more than just thoughts and hopes to create impactful narratives. To be implemented, your dreams for God can start as simple thoughts, but they will need planning and action. It's easy for any of us to talk about how we would like to be the best employee, or best student, possible for God. Those are great places to start. But the action we take toward those goals is what counts. For instance, if you are a student, are you willing to make the hard choices that are sometimes required? Making a choice between a social opportunity and spending extra time on a paper due in just a few days? Are you ready to get the extra help needed from a professor to better understand the topic at hand because you want to graduate and move forward with your degree? If you're employed, do you find yourself complaining about the lack of opportunity where you're at, or even gossiping about your new boss? Or are you actively planning your career and allowing God to open doors for how He wants to use you in your profession? Your contentment, combined with your plans and dreams, will drive the action needed toward your specific goals. The nature of this balance reflects the trust you have in God's plan for you.

God loves us more than we can imagine. His love is perfect and does not waver (Numbers 23:19, Hebrews 13:8, James 1:17). He does not take any vacation days or time off from looking over your life, nor has He from anyone else. We see throughout His Word: the effects of His blessings upon a faithful soul. We have already written about Peter, but what about John or any of the other first-century disciples who remained faithful? They would go on to tell great stories and see miraculous things as they lived their lives for God. Consider others—Noah (Genesis 6-9), Abraham (Genesis 12-23), the Ethiopian eunuch (Acts 8), the Philippian jailer (Acts 16)—all people passionate about following God. They dreamed for God. When you strive toward your dreams for God, hoping in the Lord, as Isaiah wrote, God promises you will soar! He will use you to inspire others to dream for Him. Yours will become another amazing story of God's faithfulness to His chosen people.

PREPARING TO FAIL, AND RECOGNIZING THE OPPONENT

But creating a path forward isn't easy. Even while dreaming, like the Wrights, you'll need to overcome the traps and pitfalls that can jump in your path along the way. For Orville and Wilbur Wright, their dream, at its core, was dangerous and filled with difficulty. Dreaming of what God can do through you could be hazardous as well! On the one hand, dreaming can be the very thing that catapults one's thoughts and efforts to impact the world for the better. But putting your heart and soul on the line, working hard and spending hours working toward a vision—well, this also provides a chance to fail. And defeat can be discouraging, maybe even catastrophic. A failed dream can cause a large stumble, and without the heartfelt desire to get back up again, the soul can be left crushed and a goal can die. Perseverance and grit are ingredients for a lifestyle of dreaming. Humility, openness to our Father's discipline, patience, and waiting on God are all required in the journey of dreaming for Him. And one can never forget that the nature of dreaming is inherently more difficult because it has additional obstacles that make it hard to persevere through; these come from the one who is against you. Of him, Jesus said,

> *"The thief comes only to steal and kill and destroy; I have come that they may have life, and have it to the full"* (John 10:10).

The enemy is there. He has a plan to make life harder for you; he is most definitely messing with you and your goals. He is against you, and he is lying to you. Jesus could not have put it more plainly: "steal and kill and destroy." These are strong words. The enemy loves to deflate us, to take the very air from underneath our soaring wings so we fail and come crashing down. If you want to dream for God, it is a requirement to recognize this massive opponent and find the ways the thief works against you so you can overcome. Let's take this even further.

Because he is fighting against you, this enemy will attempt to twist your priorities and relationships. That is a promise. If you're a student, our enemy loves to leave you swirling in the question of how to keep God as the first priority in your life when you have homework to do. Do you study for the test, or do you go to the church meeting? If you choose to study, does that mean God is not first in your life? How do you devote yourself to God's dream when you need to work, study, and take care of other responsibilities? Satan wants all of this to be very confusing. Whether it is homework, travel, or some other type of activity, the enemy loves to twist and confuse us concerning our priorities. When we are left in that swirl, it keeps us from being productive toward our dream. Whatever hinders you from dreaming,

God understands your difficulty. He understands you. And He is on your side.

Let's fight through and overcome! First, be willing to get help. Often, other people see us more clearly than we see ourselves. Use spiritual people to help you sort through the priority swirl so you can thrive in your relationship with God even when it is hard. God is big and has long arms to reach to and hold you. Other people can help us work through priorities to the glory of God. (Later, we will examine biblical people who had big responsibilities and many priorities outside of their "spiritual" priorities; this study will shed more light on this.)

What if you are helping others? Help your friend see his or her need for perseverance and grit. Inspire their faith in God's Word. Believe in them through their challenges. If their difficulty is a temporary situation, look on it with grace. Once again, consider the Wrights' example and the many problems they had to overcome to get the right kind of aircraft to fly. The amazing thing they did was keep their focus on the dream of flying versus getting stuck on the problems of building their plane. The small issues did not dissuade them along the path toward the success of their goal. Focus your eyes on God, His dreams for you and His will for you, and decide to never give up.

Sometimes the enemy is trying to destroy us through our thoughts. God has given you an inherent desire to do great things in a way that only you can, to dream about what you can do with Him and for Him. In God, you long to bring your entire self to the table whether you are an introvert or an extrovert, a man or a woman, and regardless of race, job, socioeconomic background, or any other personality trait or circumstance that defines you. In your heart, there is a yearning to be used by God, to be trusted by Him, and to fulfill your role as a purposeful Christian. You have a craving in your soul to feel valued by God. This is true for everyone, whether you are in the ministry, an electrician, an engineer, or simply working as unpaid mother or father. You know that God loves you deeply and sees immense value in you, so much so that He gave His Son on your behalf as a sacrifice for your sins. Because of this, you desire to be driven by that dream connected to your heart. Belittling thoughts and distracting ideas, however, get in the way. The enemy continues to fight against your hopes; he wants to crush your dreams and destroy any thoughts of changing the world for the better. These thoughts can run laps in your mind: you're too young, you don't know anything, you're not as spiritual, you're "not enough," your future is nothing special, "just do your job," "just go to class," "just go to church," "you won't have an impact anyway." These are all simply lies. Recognizing them as lies will go a long way to moving them out of the way so you can plan and act on your dream.

Maybe you have thoughts like these and are having difficulty identifying a dream because of them. Perhaps you are avoiding dreaming because of fear or a specific failure. Too often we just avoid dreaming; it's easier that way. We may have a lot of non-dreaming peers around us, and this helps justify a stagnant lifestyle. There is safety in numbers. If everyone rolls a certain way, you can feel comfortable rolling with them. It's just easier. Maybe this avoidance has been caused by fear or past hurts. Maybe you were not believed in by important people in your past. Trampled dreams are not inspiring, and they are no fun, so perhaps you avoid going back to that space again. You think extremely unhealthy thoughts. You see snarky memes online and then in your mind: "Maybe the purpose of your life is to warn others." Your thoughts move in this direction, and such a thought train resonates with you far more than healthy dreaming.

Unaccomplished goals are deflating as well. You've had inspirational ideas in the past, set hopeful goals for the year or had optimistic plans for a semester. But they weren't met. In faith, you tried again, but again you missed reaching them. You tried a *third* time, but struck out, and you aren't going back. You're tired of failure! You put up spiritual walls around you and hide in your cocoon because that is where you think happiness lies and where you can safely avoid dreams.

Perhaps you have not been thinking about your future at all, the direction your life is going, your interests, or what lies ahead. Maybe you are just unsure how to think about the future, so you ignore what is ahead. While you don't say it out loud, you still like being a kid, and the thought of taking hold of your future, having dreams and setting goals past next week, is too daunting, so you don't move forward. Thinking about your future can be intimidating, especially if doing so is a new concept for you.

INSTEAD, CHOOSE THIS: EYES ON JESUS AND LIFE TO THE FULL

For any of these reasons, and more, it is often more comfortable not to have dreams or a vision. It is easier to live life day to day, week to week, and not wish for a brighter tomorrow. The enemy is working tirelessly to stop you from dreaming for God, to steal your zest for the gifts God has given you. Remember Jesus' words: "steal and kill and destroy." Don't let yourself get tangled in a web of the enemy's lies.

Let's focus on the second part of that Scripture. Jesus says, "I have come that they may have life, and have it to the full." Let's go deeper with how Scripture can help us break out of our fears and insecurities.

> *Shortly before dawn Jesus went out to them, walking on the lake. When the disciples saw him walking on the lake, they were terrified. "It's a ghost," they said, and cried out in fear. But Jesus immediately said to them: "Take courage! It is I. Don't be afraid."*
>
> *"Lord, if it's you," Peter replied, "tell me to come to you on the water."*
>
> *"Come," he said.*
>
> *Then Peter got down out of the boat, walked on the water and came toward Jesus. But when he saw the wind, he was afraid and, beginning to sink, cried out, "Lord save me!"* (Matthew 14:25-30)
>
> *Let us fix our eyes on Jesus, the author and perfecter of our faith, who for the joy set before him endured the cross, scorning its shame, and sat down at the right hand of the throne of God* (Hebrews 12:2).

> *So we fix our eyes not on what is seen, but on what is unseen. For what is seen is temporary, but what is unseen is eternal* (2 Corinthians 4:18).

While the enemy is busy messing with you, trying to destroy you, God still has your back. It seems possible that Paul, in his letter to the church in Corinth, and the writer of Hebrews may have been thinking of Peter's night on the water. Peter inevitably hung onto that lesson himself. That night the disciples were together, just having finished another day with Jesus. They were all terrified as Jesus approached, walking on water, but it was Peter who called out. Think about what Peter asked: he knew that if it wasn't Jesus, what he was asking would not be possible. If it was Jesus, however, Peter was confident something astounding could happen. It isn't clear how many steps he took on the water, but the Bible says Peter walked toward Jesus. We all know what happens next—especially since the thief comes to steal our faith and destroy our confidence. Peter loses sight of his Lord, and the apparent problems at hand take his eyes completely away from Jesus.

To overcome the fight that the enemy will bring against you, you must look to Jesus and keep your eyes fixed there. (In chapter three, we will discuss this in more detail.) But we also want to remind you of Isaiah 40 at the beginning of this chapter, of putting your hope in the Lord. We grow weary in our fight and the enemy is relentless, it seems. But the explicit promise in God's Word is that He will sustain you if you hope in Him, if you fix your eyes on Him, and if He is the anchor to your soul. Launching into your future with God all starts here. There is no step-by-step method to dream for God without having a focus on God. Think of the Wrights: all the work toward their dream focused squarely on creating a flying machine.

You shouldn't fight this fight alone; to do so is tiresome. Surround yourself with fellow dreamers for support. Allow God to work through others around you as you battle back against the schemes of our enemy. It is so encouraging and uplifting to see others gain success, to have victories, to celebrate together. Sometimes God hands this encouragement to you, but many times it takes you reaching out to be a friend, and this can be difficult. In the same way that watching the Olympics may inspire you to begin exercising, we can be encouraged to dream by seeing fellow dreamers. Knowing this, Jesus sent out seventy-two (Luke 10) to go before Him to towns and villages nearby; this was a daunting task He gave them! He sent them out in pairs to support each other and be each other's cheerleaders. In the same way, you need helpers; you need fellow dreamers at your side engaged in their Christianity. This is how to put your future on the right footing!

Another simple step that can help you in your dreams is to write your thoughts down, talk about them, and keep them at the forefront of your mind. Whether you are a goal- or task-oriented person or not, writing things down can prove to be a tremendous aid. Then take things a step further: make a to-do list toward that end and keep it in front of you day by day, week by week. What are the details needed for you to accomplish your dreams? Go to God in prayer with your list, laying it before him. This is a sure way to put your hope in Him.

Finally, in overcoming the pitfalls, recognize the mercy and grace God has already freely given you, and reflect that to others. We have all dropped the ball, sinned against God, and hurt others along the way. But He gives us mercy; He provides us the opportunity to have those wrongs wiped away. He gives us a clean slate! When you are tempted to feel the weight of failures, insecurities, or fears, remember that the Lord has wiped your personal slate clean, that his mercies are new every morning (Lamentations 3:22, 23). In His mercy, He does not hold anything against you—so don't hold anything against yourself! It is God who has freely given us our life, our experiences, and too many blessings to count. We have received much from Him. In humility, dwell deeply on this and consider how you can pass this gift on to others.

We write this because people may inadvertently hurt you along the way even if they are trying to help. You may receive lousy advice, be on the wrong end of an accusation, or merely be sinned against in one way or another as the enemy tries to steal and kill and destroy. The enemy would love for you to focus on these things, to take your eyes away from your dreams for God. You can choose to fight back! It is our pride that often gets in the way, and it often shows itself in anger or disgust. Recognize the humanity that exists in all of us: you, your peers, simply everyone. Choosing to put your hope in the Lord, you can give grace and mercy to those around you just as it has been given to you time and time again. Trust that God has your best interest at heart, persevere against the mountains before you, and know that God will lead the way down the right path for those who remain humble.

In giving you His Son, God helps open your eyes to a clearer vision and to the impactful life He desires. Just as the sun rises each day to light your path, He has given you a renewed hope each morning. In God, know that you are a priceless treasure (Matthew 13:44-52) and that He sees you as a new creation (2 Corinthians 5:17). Just as it was for Peter, Jesus came to give you hope for a remarkable existence, to provide you vision of how God can use all of you and your talents to allow you to do amazing things. He came so you could dream. And by God's mercy and grace, you have the power to throw off the enemy's lies and embrace the strength He gave you to dream and fulfill His purpose for you.

The Wrights worked on their flyer to accomplish their dream to soar. Let's get to work on your plane. There are plans to be made and flights in your future that only you can take. It's time to soar. Time to think about what God will do through you.

Chapter Two

PREPARED BY GOD

For you created my inmost being; you knit me together in my mother's womb. I praise you because I am fearfully and wonderfully made; your works are wonderful, I know that full well. My frame was not hidden from you when I was made in the secret place. When I was woven together in the depths of the earth, your eyes saw my unformed body. All the days ordained for me were written in your book before one of them came to be. How precious to me are your thoughts, O God! How vast is the sum of them! Were I to count them, they would outnumber the grains of sand. When I awake, I am still with you (Psalm 139:13-18).

Maybe it was David's own child, or possibly one belonging to a family member. It's possible that holding a newborn baby in his arms could have triggered these thoughts from Psalm 139. As an adult, David saw God at work in his life in tremendous ways. David also recognized that God's work started in him before he saw light outside his mother's womb. He understood the omnipresence of God, and in a moment of humility, he realized that God had deeply loved him since the beginning. More than his thoughts about himself, though, he valued God's thoughts, and he was ever grateful for God's early work in his life. It doesn't take much effort to see David's thankful heart and praising soul. And this gives us perspective as we begin our look at how God has been at work in our lives from before our first breath as well.

God started early in preparing you for something great. When considering your dreams and deciding to go after your future, do not underestimate the great things God has done in you already! In David's words, He created a wonderful person in you, one woven and knit together by His own hands. The creation of a human being within a mother's womb is a miracle that is often overlooked or underappreciated. We see expecting mothers all the time; there are millions every year. Consider that within each womb, God is creating yet another piece of His glory, knitting together the start of another life, each one different and unique from the next. At one time, it was your mother who was used by God to form you. In her womb was the beginning of a remarkable creation, unique to any other human who has ever been or ever will be. Noted author Bill Bryson succinctly describes the mind-blowing physical aspect of the knitting of a human being in his book *A Short History of Nearly Everything.*

> *It starts with a single cell. The first cell splits to become two and the two become four and so on. After just forty-seven doublings, you have ten thousand trillion (10,000,000,000,000,000) cells in your body and are ready to spring forth as a human being. And every one of those cells knows exactly what to do to preserve and nurture you from the moment of conception to your last breath.*
>
> *You have no secrets from your cells. They know far more about you than you do. Each one carries a copy of the complete genetic code—the instruction manual for your body—so it knows not only how to do its job but every other job in the body. Never in your life will you have to remind a cell to keep an eye on its adenosine triphosphate levels or to find a place for the extra squirt of folic acid that's just unexpectedly turned up. It will do that for you, and millions more things besides.*[4]

Add in the individual character, the likes and dislikes, the very soul of the being that God is growing, and you can't help but pause at the sheer complexity and wonder of it. You had a spectacular start long before anyone saw your smiling face or tiny toes! And God made only one of you. Out of all the billions of people who have ever lived and live now, there is not a second one of you to be found! There is not an earlier model year, a genuinely identical twin, or an identical replacement anywhere. This fact is remarkable given the sheer numbers of humanity and the abundant displays of God's creativity.

But did God finish preparing you in your mother's womb? Hardly! God has been laboring in your life for your benefit in far-reaching ways you can't possibly understand. He has worked through a combination of your parents or guardians, friends, siblings, and a whole host of experiences throughout your life that continue to shape you and lead you to where you are today. Your kindergarten teacher had an influence, your first-grade teacher, a coach, a relative, and so on—a seemingly endless cast of influential characters helped make you who you are today. And what is wholly remarkable is this effort is not just unique to you. God continues to spearhead efforts that shape every one of your days, but also those of your neighbor, your friend, and billions of people you don't know! He is not prejudiced about His work. He is at work through all cultures and backgrounds, through every state and county, and through every country that covers the earth. The creation story did not end in Genesis. It continues to this day and will go on tomorrow as the world grows more colorful and more miraculous with each growing soul. God is an amazing craftsman.

> *This is the word that came to Jeremiah from the Lord: "Go down to the potter's house, and there I will give you my message." So I went down to the potter's house, and I saw him working at the wheel. But the pot he was shaping from the clay was marred in his hands; so the potter formed it into another pot, shaping it as seemed best to him. Then the word of the Lord came to me: "O house of Israel, can I not do with you as this potter does?" declares the Lord. "Like clay in the hand of the potter, so are you in my hand, O house of Israel"* (Jeremiah 18:1-6).

> *Yet, O Lord, you are our Father. We are the clay, you are the potter; we are all the work of your hand* (Isaiah 64:8).

The pictures we receive from Jeremiah and Isaiah are quite fitting. The vision of a potter at the wheel turning his pot, shaping it into a marvelous work, is a great example of God's "hands-on" intimacy. And just as Jeremiah spoke, and wrote, God's shaping is an endless process of work and rework on our behalf. The fact that God has been so involved in our lives from the start should captivate us! His continued work should give us confidence in what we can offer the world around us. Be excited about His handiwork in you! Let God's involvement in your life support your dreams and stimulate you to deliberate action. God's involvement is like having a perfect mentor to guide and coach you. The behind-the-scenes work, the interactions, relationships, jobs, and day-to-day happenings—these are all reasons to praise God that He is shaping your life. As both Jeremiah and Isaiah wrote, God will carry on with the task of developing you, regardless of your age!

SEEING GOD PAST THE ENEMY

But through the enemy's lies and distractions, we may underappreciate—or possibly not even see—the good God has done for us. Sometimes we have such difficult circumstances (serious illness, addiction, abuse, death in the family) that we find it extremely challenging to see God past the enemy. Our adversary maneuvers to distract and discourage us, causing frustration, despair, and stealing any notion of dreaming! The enemy stifles us with lies and misinformation, and we find ourselves oblivious to what a fantastic story we have from God! As we experience disappointment, failure, and yes, even tragedy, we can get caught in a circle of self-focused thought, doubt, fear, and faithlessness. We get mad at the world and sometimes even God. We lose hope, and life slowly fades to a basic existence. After that downward trail, we are leaving little to no impact. And this is just as the enemy has planned.

Maybe your struggle isn't just seeing how Satan works, it's finding a way forward past a tragic situation that throws you back to your past. You may feel chained to your past by abuse, addiction, or other challenges, and you are not sure how to navigate your way around those deep obstacles. As you go through this book, we want you to know we are committed to praying for our readers. We want you to know you are heard, you are important, and you are valued by the creator of the universe! No matter what tragedies may have happened in your life, we believe God has put a value and purpose in you that is precious, even sacred. We know that you can overcome through God. You are not alone. In chapters to come, we will bring you the victories of both regular people and our spiritual predecessors to give you a vision and a hope from God.

We encourage you to practice identifying the lies and putting them aside, simply surrendering them to God. God understands and can work with any of us regardless of our past struggles, challenges, and tragedies. When we turn to God in deep Bible study and prayer, putting our entire broken lives in front of Him, He supports us as we dream, plan, and launch our lives. You will see God work. Take time to reflect and perhaps journal the ways God has worked through your past, even in the challenging circumstances.

To further illustrate how God has been preparing you, let's look more closely at an Old Testament story. Let's shine a spotlight on how He worked in young David's life to prepare him for what was to come.

DAVID AND THE BEAR

David's father, Jesse, was from Bethlehem in Judah, from the direct family line of Abraham. He was proud of his family heritage and had a strong belief in his God, deep convictions that anchored him. His father taught David well, especially to believe in the Lord God Almighty and to devote himself to following His laws.

Some considered the young man David conceited, or a bit arrogant—a criticism that might have been warranted. He was a talented lad who was also noted to be handsome and had a developing presence about himself. David had several older brothers, so there were times he had to stick up for himself. Whether being disrespected as a young boy or just being the youngest sibling and a nuisance to his brothers, he no doubt often found himself in situations where he felt it was him against the world. But David was not known to back down. Despite all this, he also maintained a growing respect for others around him. He respected his father and his family and was grateful for all he had. He was thankful for learning how to play the harp and lyre and being able to sing songs and hymns. He was good enough at his music that people wanted to listen to him. He was even grateful for the opportunity to take care of his father's animals. It was hard work, but the animals made him laugh and gave him perspective as well. Mostly, he found simple satisfaction in taking care of them.

But of all things David considered in his life, he was most grateful for God. Although young, he had a mature respect for God. Often he would sit on a rock and think about God, reason with himself about God being Almighty and his forever-caretaker. He would consider how there was safety and security in God, and it drove him closer to his creator and helped him gain confidence and be content.

He was unique in that he loved to play music while watching the sheep, and the others would listen to him play. On occasion, a sheep or two would wander off from the rest, and either he or one of the others would tend to it, guiding it back to the flock. Having one walk away always created a dangerous moment; there was always safety in numbers from the neighboring predators. The older shepherds told stories from the field. How brave they had been to fight off a fox, or how stubborn one sheep could be against another. Sometimes, the storytellers would inflate the story in attempt to elevate their stature. The shepherds would embellish the danger or the fear, maybe even add highlights that no one would be able to disprove. True or not, the stories would often go on too long, and the old-timers would bore him to death while talking, mostly, to themselves. It was all in good jest, though, and overall, David admired their work. He loved being out there with them. It gave him a chance to dream, play his music, and write his thoughts.

On one particular day, the sheep had been doing well. They were well fed and grazing in the sun. Earlier in the morning, the young man had left with a few others to tend the flock, and, as usual, brought his lyre. He had been sent by his father for the express purpose of checking on the rest of the shepherds who were out in the fields and to bring some of the sheep back. It was a bit of a trip, taking him nearly a day to make the trek to where the sheep grazed. He often had to do some of the hardest, loneliest work to earn his stripes. But David also often found the work fun; he understood that being patient and working hard was his role for now. He was growing, and while sometimes at odds with his older brothers, the young man was soon to face a battle he would never forget.

David reached the main herds, checked with the others, and assembled the smaller herd. It was later in the day, but he then left with his sheep and planned to return to his father at home sometime the next day. The path was familiar. He and the others had been in this area before and knew it well. Beginning to weary from the day, he moved the smaller herd forward on a hillside as he kept watch.

He never saw it coming from his left, and David had only seen one of these beasts, from a distance, his entire life. The bear was startled as it saw David and his sheep reach the hill's peak. The bear had been wandering on the other side of the peak for some time and David found it just as the sun was retreating for the day. Naturally, the huge animal quickly charged at the sheep; David was shocked. In a moment, David's thoughts transpired from joy and anticipation of a beautiful setting sun to sudden panic and fear—whether it was for the sheep or himself, he screamed in horror.

David had never even *heard* of such an attack. In a desperate effort to save the sheep from the attack, he ran at the bear and swung his cane at the oncoming beast, but the weight and momentum of the animal knocked him to the ground. He was at the bear's mercy and already underneath him. In a scramble, and swinging and shouting as much as he could, David was able to beat at the bear's head with his cane, diverting the animal just enough. This allowed him to roll away and get back on his feet. The bear stood on its back legs and let out a massive roar; it was as if every living thing around the land must have heard it. David was shaken but had only one choice, and that was to fight. The sheep ran. The bear stood ten, nearly eleven cubits, and its head and paws were enormous. But all that didn't really matter—David was fighting for his life. The beast, seeing David as its opponent and now ignoring the sheep, stood and roared a second time, daring David to make a move. David stood in a fighting stance with his knees bent, cane at the ready; he had learned the position from one of his older brothers. At the time, however, he had learned only in fun with the idea of fighting off a fox.

A third time, the bear let out a thunderous roar and then charged. David jumped to a rock about waist high and took another swing at the bear with the cane; the lyre was laying on the ground nearby, probably broken. The cane was only a small deterrent, and its only accomplishment was to further anger the bear. David's left leg had a bleeding scrape and his left arm was bleeding as well. These were among other bruises from the initial charge, though David didn't notice the others. David had never experienced this amount of adrenaline before; he had no time to feel the pain. Somehow, though, he knew he was bleeding. The two were alone to settle their dispute. The bear roared in anger and tried to reach David's head, arms, or any part he could bite or tear to shreds with its jaw. In a flash, David found himself behind the bear, on its back, and he clung to the behemoth; he was able to wrap his right arm around the bear's neck. He knew he needed to stay on the beast's back to avoid the ferocious jaws and savage claws. The bear fought to rid itself of this stranglehold—jarring movement, jumping, roaring in anger, but now it was beginning to struggle with fatigue. David held on for his life. As seconds passed, David sensed that he possibly now had the upper hand. He hung on until he was finally able to wrestle the bear to the ground, the animal gasping for air. Quickly, David grabbed a smaller rock, about the size of his hand, lying nearby, with his left hand; his right still clung to the neck of the beast that was now fighting for its own life.

It took several swings at the bear's head with the rock to finally beat it to unconsciousness, and the wilting roars faded to silence. David stood, gasping for air himself, and now threw the rock directly at its head in anger and determination. He then found a larger rock nearby that could finally finish the bear. In exhaustion, David sat on the ground, crumbling in emotion. He was the victor. He had killed the bear with his own hands.

As the skies darkened, David, dirty and full of scrapes and gouges from the bear claws, did his best to bandage his legs. He hobbled over to find his bag and lyre; he let the broken cane lay. He mustered enough energy to gather the sheep and return to the path that led home. The exhausted and injured David would continue making his way home into the night. He had not lost one sheep.

> *But David said to Saul, "Your servant has been keeping his father's sheep. When a lion or a bear came and carried off a sheep from the flock, I went after it, struck it and rescued the sheep from its mouth. When it turned on me, I seized it by its hair, struck it and killed it. Your servant has killed both the lion and the bear; this uncircumcised Philistine will be like one of them, because he has defied the armies of the living God. The Lord who delivered me from the paw of the lion and the paw of the bear will deliver me from the hand of this Philistine"* (1 Samuel 17:34-37).

The story that plays out in 1 Samuel 17 is spectacular, and we can draw much from a quick review. David probably had no idea God was preparing him when he faced the ferocious animals. Perhaps the scenes with the bear and lion unfolded in a manner similar to the story we've relayed here—or not. Regardless, what is undeniable is that David, while still in his teens, had handled both a lion and bear, two monstrous animals. Instead of feeling like a lonely shepherd boy who had these two terrible moments that he somehow survived, David saw clearly. He saw these victories as God's love for him, God's preparation for him for future battles. At this moment with Saul, David reminded

Saul, and perhaps himself, that he had miraculously defeated these animals and was now ready for the Philistine, Goliath, who jeered the Israelite army. David, still a teenager, reasoned with the king that, despite his youth, he could defeat the enemy that no other adult man in the Israelite army was willing to battle. David saw this obstacle as a conquerable one, and he saw how God had prepared him. Knowing God was with him convinced him not to worry.

YOUR BEAR, YOUR GIANT

In the same way, God's preparation of you has included difficult tasks. You have had battles to fight, maybe more than you'd wished. And while it is easier to hide in fear, denial, or apathy, the battles don't go away. They are lessons to prepare you for dreaming and soaring. Your battles sit in front of you, waiting for your next move, just like a certain Philistine giant and his army. If you are in college, you may be close to finishing, but you also may be feeling scared of what is to come. Where will I go? What will I do? Where will I work? You may be uncertain of a new city, a new church, or a new ministry. If you have started your career, and you look at the long and daunting road ahead, you may be wondering what you want to be "when you grow up"! You've had skirmishes on the battlegrounds of relationships, friends who were once close have moved on, and you may have earned friendship wounds along the way. Your new dating relationship is not the Hallmark Channel movie you had hoped for—or maybe it is—but you still fear what may lie ahead. Or, all your friends are getting married, except for you, and the enemy is lying to you. Doubts and disappointments seemingly surround you; they cloud your eyes and keep you from seeing that God is at work on your behalf, even through the shadows of darkness. The battles are everywhere, and uncertainty can wreak havoc on both your contentment and your faith. Through all this, you may be feeling like you're being called to rely on God. It's just plain hard.

A closer look at 1 Samuel 17 and the events that unfolded before

David that day reveal a parallel to four different foes we may face today.

1) The Israelite Army: Status Quo

The Israelite army had come with the intention of fighting against the Philistines in Judah, about fifteen miles from David's home. They had enjoyed previous victories, but now they sat before their rivals doubtful and filled with trepidation. What David saw in the Israelite camp was a sad and hopeless situation in which the army, including some of his brothers, was just plain afraid. These were grown men fearing what they saw and choosing to stand still. Unified in their fear, the status quo of the group was to do nothing, or, if anything, to run. If anyone had a renegade thought of meeting Goliath, no doubt simple logic applied by the others would have dissuaded him. *Who am I? I can't do it. I'm going to stick with the norm. I don't want to rock the boat.*

If one man asked another to join him, they talked each other out of it. Their spirits were disheartened, their faith had badly waned, and the downward spiral had taken over. Abstaining from any action at all caused their faith to dip even lower. Whatever training the Israelites had and whatever their fighting experience, there was not one of them who felt confident to face this enemy. They did not see themselves as prepared for this battle. They all knew it and acted accordingly. The army even had great incentive to fight against Goliath and the Philistines! Great wealth and the king's daughter were the rewards offered to the man who would gird up his loins and fight—but none took the offer. They were God's chosen but were at a standstill, unwilling to pick up their swords against the Philistines. This deadlock lasted nearly a month and a half with no one willing to step forward and make a difference. At its core, the army was content to stay fearful and satisfied with its complacency. Today, it may seem somewhat difficult to believe that no one could muster the courage to make the situation different—until the young David came along.

We have similar struggles, falling in with the status quo and settling for less. The spirit of complacency and satisfaction can cause long delays, even stop our dreams. When we are not engaged and not determined to focus on what is ahead, we can find ourselves in a swirl of self-inflicted defeat. We starve ourselves of inspiration. Fighting against complacency is a daily battle. Each day brings new challenges, and each day is another chance for the enemy to keep you in that downward swirl and forgetting about your dream to soar. Additionally, when an army of the complacent, those settling for less, without any intention to follow through on dreams, surrounds us, it becomes even more difficult to rise up and be a dreamer. This world urgently needs more men and women like David. Do not be swayed by the non-dreamers around you. Stand up, keep working on your plane! God has prepared you to fly!

2) King Saul: Doubt from Disobedience

At the head of this fearful army, Saul was the commander of the Israelites, and he led the way only in apprehension. When Goliath made his taunts, Saul stood with his men, unable to muster the confidence in God needed to fight the giant. He knew about the experienced Goliath and he knew he was big. Saul had faced a slew of opponents in the time since he had become ruler over Israel. By the power of God, he had punished the Ammonites as well as defeating Moab and Edom and routing other kings as well! With God as Saul's source of strength, he had previously triumphed over the Philistines, a bitter enemy whenever there were ongoing battles. Saul had fought bravely and valiantly against many enemies in the past. But now, well, this was a different Saul. This Saul struggled, and he did not have the fearless confidence God had once given him. His prior success led him to his choice of disobedience to God (1 Samuel 15), a decision he would never overcome. Further, he simply doubted. He doubted his army would be victorious over Goliath and the Philistines. He doubted God. And he doubted David.

> *David said to Saul, "Let no one lose heart on account of the Philistine; your servant will go and fight him." Saul replied, "You*

> *are only a boy, and he [Goliath] has been a fighting man from his youth"* (1 Samuel 17:32, 33).

Doubt can be a real stumbling block. It clouds dreams and leads us to open waters with no destination in sight. With no direction, we find ourselves in a storm of doubt from which it seems impossible to flee. It comes from two places: others around us, and our own minds. There is a heavy influence of persuasion when a neighbor or friend doubts our abilities. We feel it, and it can come when we least expect it; it can come through something like a small comment or a noticeable eyeroll. The doubters do not give us confidence. They provide us with uncertainty. They fill us with hesitation and insecurity. Their words or actions toward us can take what we dreamed and believed possible and make it impossible. The world camps here; it's a dark and pessimistic place. There is little positivity. This environment fuels your doubt in yourself and your doubt in God as well.

And then we can struggle with hesitation, pulling back in our minds, telling ourselves what we can't do and what we can't accomplish. It's a battle, but you can fight against this negativity. Saul's biggest problem was his disobedience to God that caused his confidence to fade. He took his eyes away from God. For any of us, our best help is to walk deeply with God with a heart to obey and be humble. Additionally, choose to be confident with yourself and especially with, and around, others. Meditate on how God has prepared you, and even though you don't know the road ahead, be assured God's hand is with you.

And, of course, encourage others. Be deliberate in telling them they are amazing and what you appreciate about them. Hearten their dreams to fly! It is amazing how quickly you can make a friend when you are encouraging.

3) Goliath, the Armor, and the Philistine Army: The Case to Not Dream

To the Philistines' credit, they sought to end this standoff. Twice a day they would attempt to end the battle as Goliath, a proud warrior, would bravely step to the front to meet an opponent. He would taunt and call them names; no doubt he had a booming, gruff voice. The Philistine hero looked terrifying. The description of him we read is quite extraordinary.

> *He had a bronze helmet on his head and wore a coat of scale armor of bronze weighing five thousand shekels [about 125 pounds], on his legs he wore bronze greaves [plate armor for the leg], and a bronze javelin was slung on his back. His spear shaft was like a weaver's rod, and its iron point weighed six hundred shekels [about 15 pounds]. His shield bearer went ahead of him* (1 Samuel 17:5-7).

No wonder the Israelite army was so unsure. It's probably fair to say that just the armor and weaponry he carried was enough for the Israelites to step back in fear. He was covered with armor from head to toe and backed by the entire Philistine army. It made the mountain of victory seem too tall to climb! The Israelites could not see a single part of the man that was vulnerable. Additionally, Goliath had a colleague, presumably shorter but also very strong, in front of him for the sole purpose of carrying his shield! The whole scene created a powerful vision in which no Israelite thought victory possible. Any hope of an attack was drowned out by what they saw and heard.

Isn't that just like our enemy, creating a dark vision of being dominated that thwarts any hope we have of gaining victory in our battles? In the last chapter, we discussed how our opponent lies, distracts, and is out to get us, to "steal and kill and destroy." What does he do to you personally, and who does he work through to steal your dreams? How does he do it? He is out to make you think you can't do it; he is out to convince you that you are a failure. He makes you think your battles will be fine left as is, that there is no reasonable hope for you to win. He hates you and wants to stomp out any confidence. He doesn't want you to soar—ever.

But just as God gave David victory, you can be assured He is helping you as well. He hasn't prepared you to look at your battles. He has prepared you to fight them, to be victorious, to live a life of impact.

4) The Brothers: Relational Headwinds

David had at least seven older brothers, some of which were tall and impressive, especially Eliab. Eliab was noteworthy enough that the great prophet Samuel, on first seeing him, thought he was the one to be anointed king of the Israelites and eventually replace the fading Saul. After God rejected Eliab, David's father brought in the rest of the older brothers for Samuel to consider as king. Once again, though, at God's direction, Samuel did not choose any of them. It was finally David—an initial afterthought—who was appointed as the future king. There were undoubtedly sibling battles before this time, and David's anointing probably served to drive a deeper wedge between him and at least some of his brothers. This wedge showed itself even more deeply when David came to the Israelite army asking about Goliath and the Philistines.

> *When Eliab, David's oldest brother, heard him speaking with the men, he burned in anger at him and asked, "Why have you come down here? And with whom did you leave those few sheep in the desert? I know how conceited you are and how wicked your heart is; you came down only to watch the battle"* (1 Samuel 17:28).

They had the same father, the same bloodline, and of all the relationships David had at this battlefront, surely his family would have been among his best and most supportive! But Eliab was angry, and he let David have a public lashing. He disrespected David and made false accusations about him in front of the men. Eliab questioned David's heart and his purpose. Behind it, there was unquestionably a heart of jealousy and bitterness.

In our battles to dream for God, to strive to be used by God in any way He sees fit, sometimes it's the people closest to us who are the least supportive, or those who simply hurt us the most. Perhaps his own brother's comments were the most hurtful. As we discussed in chapter one, it is critical to have mercy and much grace in your tool belt and to keep your eyes fixed on God. Eliab's eyes had nothing but anger for David; he mouthed off concerns about a few sheep and spouted accusations against his younger brother. David, an impeccable example for us, kept his eyes focused on God. He remained focused on God while Eliab and all of those around him were looking elsewhere.

Whether God caused the bear and lion to attack, or simply allowed them to, doesn't matter. It was a hard training ground for David, but one that enabled him to do great things later in life. Having already been anointed by God to become king of Israel, David was on his way to greatness. Very few, however, knew that yet. David, still just a teenager, could not see anything that God *couldn't* do, and he was particularly upset that Goliath would dishonor the living God. He remembered how God had prepared him for that moment and later saw how God had been preparing him his entire life. This moment would change the course of so many lives. It would set the course for the Israelites to reach for greater heights in their faith and trust in God. The stone that David slung at Goliath to kill him would mark the start of an incredible story of faith, relationship, patience, and endurance. Ironically, his remarkable action would also cause damaging, counterproductive thoughts in the current king and expose that king's selfishness. But David's powerful moments have inspired millions of people for more than three thousand years.

HOW HAS GOD PREPARED YOU?

Have you considered how God has prepared you? What victories have you gained; what defeats have you endured? What talents have you been given? No one knows what the future holds, but seeing that God has prepared you is the key to moving into the life God has planned for you. You can confidently know that God is at work. Consider David, or Peter, who we discussed earlier. These men were not aware of all that was ahead of them, but they did entrust themselves to God and His will. God prepared them to be strong in ways unique to them. And just as it was for them, it will be a continual process for you as well. His love and His plans will never stop coming your way.

Without any doubt, God has made you unique in this world, and that is for the world's benefit. Regardless of your background, your history, or your personality, God has a plan and a dream for you. The world needs your bright smile and maybe that funny laugh to make it more loving. It needs your willingness to help and your compassionate giving to help meet needs. It needs your leadership skills and your successes for the betterment of humanity. It needs your hurts and mistakes to draw others to you to learn about God's healing. It needs your positive and negative experiences that allow you to be vulnerable, kind, and relatable. It needs your realness, your authenticity, so others don't feel they must be perfect. It needs your faith in God for inspiration, your grace and mercy, and your talents in what you do best. It needs your love of the arts, your passion for family, your athletic abilities, and your cooking skills as well! It needs your education, your degree, your tremendous people skills. It needs all the unique things God has willed to you. It needs you to live an inspired life, it needs your dreams, and you can do it.

Don't underestimate yourself; you are invaluable. You are a wonderfully strong and powerful human being who has a presence that God has given the world. There is not another you! You are the only one who can fulfill the role God has offered you, and He has been preparing you for some time.

Open your eyes, dream about your future, and go after it. Assemble your plane and look to the open skies! Dream to soar, to soar like an eagle. God is continuing to prepare you for your story of greatness.

Chapter Three

THE FOUNDATION FORMULA

He has showed you, O Man, what is good. And what does the Lord require of you? To act justly and to love mercy and to walk humbly with your God (Micah 6:8).

Buildings need firm foundations to stand. In earlier days, builders used cut stones or rocks to create the most stability they could, but the nineteenth-century invention of Portland cement enabled sturdier, longer-lasting footholds that we see in construction today. Foundations, either literal or figurative, are critical to sustaining anything long term. Jesus told a simple parable about this with the house built on the rock versus the house built on sand (Matthew 7:24-27). In that case, the foundation Jesus referenced was the context of putting God's work into practice in our lives. It stands to reason, then, that your relationship with God, your walking with God, is the primary thing that will help in the challenges, chaos, uncertainty, and emotions that will come as you launch your life and your dreams for God.

Just down the road from our home, there is a newly planned retail center on which construction has been started. You have probably passed construction sites while driving; they can cause a sort of quiet anticipation of things to come. At the beginning of any construction process, the ground is graded and leveled, the soil tested, and then it is prepared for the digging of the foundation. The construction workers at the retail center near our home, it seemed, spent weeks moving the dirt on the right to the left side, and the dirt on the left side over to the right, but in the end they left clear, level areas for the construction of this collection of retail buildings. If you are reading this book at home, in a coffee shop, or in some other type of structure, you have probably not even thought about whether the building you are sitting in will come crashing down. You are quite secure in the groundwork and foundation that was planned and executed at the beginning of construction. The foundation holds you secure and unshaken; it keeps you safe without a thought. It is the most critical part of any building. Ironically, at the end of a construction process, no one looks at a beautiful home or office building and thinks about how great the foundation is! We look at the landscaping, the beautiful front door, the windows, and how the outside ties together with the inside to make a comfortable, attractive space. We don't think about what is underground, the very thing that keeps the pretty stuff above looking pretty! The foundation work is not flashy, yet it requires detailed installation. It is the basis for all the other items we see.

As you consider your future, build your life ahead upon a foundation planted firmly on God, the Rock. For real security, there is just no other option. Without the constant engagement of our heart, soul, and energy toward the Lord and His work, our foundation will crack. Over time, just as with a home or office building, a cracked foundation can lead to further damage and higher costs. Without deliberate effort toward building and sustaining a solid foundation, we face the danger of growing older and becoming more reliant on ourselves and our knowledge and life experiences and less reliant on God. This path can involve days spent without meaningful time with God in prayer or Bible study. We might then see our days actually turn out OK, so we unconsciously see a lesser need for depending on God.

Without thinking, we can buy into the self-reliant and self-focused lies of our enemy. Our ministry fades, we become churchgoers, and we leave it to others to be church growers. Time passes since we first made Jesus the Lord of our lives and were so grateful to have such great friends in the church. And while we know we shouldn't, we can slowly grow numb to the cross, sometimes unknowingly so. We are not quick to forgive when someone hurts us, and these very hurts can etch away at our relationship with God. While we still attend on Sunday mornings, our priorities start to differ from God's priorities, and we stop dreaming of what we can do for God. We begin to find security in planning for homes, status, career, savings and investment accounts, or other relationships, and not in God. Even when we read God's Word, we can feel numb, and the great stories of faith do not impact us as they used to. They don't call us higher; they remain only great stories to read. Our knowledge carries us, and our opinions serve us well, so we rely on them. Our dream for *God* fades while *our* dream emerges. Do you find yourself struggling in any of these types of situations? Do they strike a nerve? Or is there something else that takes your heart away from God? It can happen.

But there is always hope.

We should learn from Peter. He had several moments in which he fell short in his relationship with Jesus. There were times he had good intentions about having a strong foundation, but the plans, when tested, proved to be shallow and weak. In chapter one, we discussed his moment on the water; the other disciples were behind him in the boat.

> *Then Peter got down out of the boat, walked on the water and came toward Jesus. But when he saw the wind, he was afraid and, beginning to sink, cried out, "Lord, save me!"* (Matthew 14:29, 30)

It was amazing that Peter even stepped out of the boat. Imagine the others watching him; they had to be stunned! Here he was, a guy who grew up fishing on these very waters, a fisherman who had spent countless nights trying to make his living. He certainly never dreamed of an encounter like this. The moment would not end victoriously for him, but rather as a hard lesson in staying focused on his Lord.

And then there was this moment. Among others, this was maybe his most noted time of collapsing faith, again exposing a flawed foundation.

> *Peter replied, "Man, I don't know what you're talking about!" Just as he was speaking, the rooster crowed. The Lord turned and looked straight at Peter. Then Peter remembered the word the Lord had spoken to him: "Before the rooster crows today, you will disown me three times." And he went outside and wept bitterly* (Luke 22:60-62).

Shortly before his third denial of Jesus, Peter had fervently come to his Lord's defense. His adrenaline welled up as Jesus was arrested, so much so that he drew a sword and was willing to fight for Jesus. But the situation became increasingly more difficult, more intense as the night progressed, and with it came another test of Peter's foundation. In a familiar ending, Peter became preoccupied with his circumstances. The winds and waves were too much for him once again, his faith waned, and his foundation failed. Luke records that it was Jesus who looked at Peter, and we might imagine that Peter's eyes once again drifted elsewhere. In three separate moments that evening, he flatly denied even knowing Jesus.

Thirty years later, perhaps it was these lessons and others that were still fresh in Peter's mind as he neared the end of his life. In his second letter, he wrote about the effort it would take to overcome the enemy's lies and the corruption the world offers. His encouragement was not to give up but to keep building a foundation strong enough to overcome the tests that come our way.

> *For this reason, make every effort to add to your faith goodness; and to goodness, knowledge; and to knowledge, self-control; and to self-control, perseverance; and to perseverance, godliness; and to godliness, brotherly kindness; and to brotherly kindness, love. For if you possess these qualities in increasing measure, they will keep you from being ineffective and unproductive in your knowledge of our Lord Jesus Christ* (2 Peter 1:5-8).

Similar to Peter, you also will have your focus tested. There will be many distractions that preoccupy your mind, diverting your attention from Jesus and your relationship with God and the time you spend with Him. Remember that our enemy is out to "steal, kill and destroy." His unending efforts to bring you down are the very reasons it is so important that you deliberately and humbly walk with your God, building a strong foundation as you carefully consider and plan your future. Peter's call for each of us to be intentional and devoted is for our benefit in enhancing our faith and growing our relationship with God. Leave the distractions behind to focus on Jesus as you dream about the future. Whether you are an educator, salesperson, or waitress, resolve to be a giver, just as Jesus was, and develop your own mustard seed of faith. Offer it to God and see what He can do. And listen to Peter's plea, from experience, to "make every effort." Dream for God; there are big plans that lie ahead.

With this in mind, let's look at the ingredients needed to build our foundation formula: prayer, Bible study, and personal ministry.

PRAYER

At the start of Luke 11, we see Jesus in prayer. Upon finishing, His disciples come to Him and asked Him to teach them to pray. Have you ever wondered why they did that? After all, is that a question you have ever thought of asking someone? Is prayer something more than the folding of hands, the closing of the eyes, and simply talking to God? The disciples may have seen the religious leaders and churchgoers of their time pray, but there was something *different* in Jesus, something they had never seen before. The disciples regularly saw Jesus in prayer, and it became apparent to them how important it was to their Master. Jesus drew His strength and security from praying, and He let that time with God set His course. This was plainly visible to His disciples. In verses 2-4 of this chapter, Jesus teaches His followers details of prayer, including topics they ought to bring to God. In verses 5-13, however, Luke spends much more time recording Jesus' teaching on how God *answers* our prayers. Perhaps the disciples had spent time in prayer before, but it just didn't seem like God was answering their requests, or maybe it felt like God wasn't there. Perhaps they weren't experiencing the results to meet their expectations. It is interesting to consider that the disciples' inquiry about how to pray comes after watching Jesus pray! They weren't asking these questions while Jesus was talking to them about prayer. He was in the act of praying; He was setting the standard once again as He often did! In this example from Jesus, we see His prayer life providing a higher call to His disciples, and they wanted to figure out how He did it. They wanted the details because there was something there they saw making a difference for Jesus.

In a teaching opportunity sometime after the Luke 11 account, Jesus instructs His disciples more deeply on prayer.

> *Then Jesus told his disciples a parable to show them that they should always pray and not give up. He said: "In a certain town there was a judge who neither feared God nor cared about men. And there was a widow in that town who kept coming to him with the plea, 'Grant me justice against my adversary.' For some time he refused. But finally he said to himself, 'Even though I don't fear God or care about men, yet because this widow keeps bothering me, I will see that she gets justice, so that she won't eventually wear me out with her coming!'" And the Lord said, "Listen to what the unjust judge says. And will not God bring about justice for his chosen ones, who cry out to him day and night? Will he keep putting them off? I tell you, he will see that they get justice, and quickly. However, when the Son of Man comes, will he find faith on the earth?"* (Luke 18:1-8)

Luke puts it plainly in verse one. Jesus told this parable because He knew His disciples would be tempted to give up during prayer. It applies to us as well, and Jesus knew this. We need this parable to remind us to keep praying and not give up. Deep, meaningful, and persistent prayer challenges our faith. We know His word teaches us that He is attentive, but we don't always see the answers to our prayers, especially in the timing we think is appropriate (or needed). We see in

Jesus' illustration, also known as the Parable of the Persistent Widow, that the widow is continually coming back to the judge and crying out for justice. Jesus is quick to note her passion, her persistence, and her mind-set of refusing to give up in a situation far from ideal. It took extra effort. Jesus teaches how God longs to bless His chosen ones through prayer.

Interestingly, the last sentence of the parable shifts to ask the question: "When the Son of Man comes, will He find faith on the earth?" This statement can seem out of place with the rest of the story. Hadn't Jesus just been talking about prayer and not giving up? It seems as though Jesus is trying to help us to fight through the faith challenges that bring the discouragement that dulls our prayer life. It is the persistent widow in Jesus' parable who sets an example for us of what faith should look like in our prayers. Do we continue to go back to God, day after day, or is our "faith limit" reached under challenging circumstances? Is prayer our path for a healthy outlet for our emotions? It can be hard to ask God to help us process our emotions to get to a place of obedience. On the one hand, we can pray the hard, difficult prayers of vulnerability and gut-level honesty with God. On the other hand, we can limit our relationship with God by not moving through those emotions to a place of obedience in surrendering those emotions and circumstances to God's will. Without that surrender and trust, what can feel like an emotional and bonding prayer life can be misleading. Our prayer lives can be more reflective of living by our emotions than showing reliance on God through surrender, trust, and obedience to Him and His Word.

Do our prayers have the passion, loud cries, and spirit of never giving up? Does the Son of Man find faith in your prayers today? Does your spouse or roommate see persistence or discouragement in your prayers? What inspiration are you providing?

We see Jesus in prayer as a lifestyle many times throughout the gospels. In Mark 1:35, after a tremendously long day of giving and serving the needy, we see Jesus rising before first light to go pray by Himself. It seems the others were still sleeping. Later, His disciples became quite anxious because they could not find Him. Simon finally spots Jesus and tells Him, "Everyone is looking for you!" So we see that Jesus has been praying for quite some time, long before anyone has awakened. His time with God is enough for Him to reshift His focus onto the journey that lay ahead of these men.

Our prayer time is a barometer of our faith, a measuring stick of our relationship with God. Consider the example of Jesus in the Garden of Gethsemane the night before He would go to the cross. There was not a more emotional and challenging time for Jesus than that evening. He had probably been praying about this moment for some time. So He spent much of that night wrestling in prayer. He had read the prophecy in Isaiah and knew what was coming. The disciples, exhausted from sorrow (Luke 22:45), fell asleep. They left Jesus by Himself to pray. Only God was with Him, and Jesus had confidence in that fact. Luke 22:43 says an angel was with Him and strengthened Him in this moment. Jesus was no doubt lonely and yet with God; sad, yet joy was ahead of Him. Jesus didn't give up. He was faithful in prayer until the end.

Despite the constant needs of the poor, the hungry, the sick, and having disciples to teach, Jesus developed a healthy and crucial need to stay connected with God in prayer for absolute strength and sustenance. Even though He was God himself, Jesus knew He could not accomplish this monumental task alone. As humans, we often think we can function spiritually without time with God. But even Jesus set boundaries that allowed Him to be spiritually fed. How much more do we need to set limits on our time, our social media, our phone, so that we can tap into the strength and life that comes only from staying deeply connected to our Father.

Consider also the changes in the disciples' lives before and after Jesus was with them. While we do not know much about their lives before meeting Jesus, we learn that they didn't know much about prayer. Jesus taught them to pray as part of their faith. Did they get it? Did they learn to pray? Yes! The disciples' faith after Jesus left the earth is both inspirational and astonishing. Their foundation had been built well; it was strong. In Acts 1, Jesus was no longer with them physically. There was uncertainty, plenty of questions, and the faith of the followers of Jesus had not been tested like this before. Before this time, these emotions, this situation, likely would have yielded different results. But now, we see them faithfully going to their God in prayer (in both verse 14 and again in verse 24). They now knew how to pray, they knew prayer was needed, and they weren't giving up. Think about Peter. He must have grasped how he needed a strong prayer life for his foundation to help keep his eyes focused on God. Prayer had become a priority to him and the rest because that was the example Jesus had set for them.

In Acts, we find that, again and again, the disciples are praying, or praying and fasting, as their faith and trust in God continues to grow. In addition to Acts 1, read Acts 2:42; 3:23, 24; 4:31; 9:40; 10:2; 12:5, 12; 13:3; 14:23; 16:25; 20:36; and 21:5. But this movement of prayer didn't stop with the followers we see in Acts 1. Many of Paul's letters contain references to prayer, and one can see how important that time was to the early Christian faith. The disciples had learned why they needed prayer, they learned to be persistent, and they most certainly cried out aloud from time to time. They had watched Jesus, and their prayers simply became a reflection of their faith and reliance on God, the building of a strong foundation. Do others see your prayers impacting your life like it did the disciples? Does anyone know what you are praying or if you are praying? Do they know about your longer, more persistent prayers? Do you actively share your answered prayers? Do you direct others to actively pray about the difficulties in their lives? When considering how to spread your inspiration and your dreams to soar, you can have a profound impact on those around you by spending great time in prayer and humbly sharing with others. God is amazing. Feel free to discuss how He is alive in your life!

The Bible is also clear that God answers prayer. In Genesis 18–19, we see a story in which God not only answers a prayer need; we see how He does it. The ancient city of Sodom had descended to a horrible place in which to live. It had a sick culture and perversion, and likewise, with neighboring city Gomorrah, God had declared to destroy both places because of the sin. Abraham's nephew Lot was living in Sodom trying to live a more righteous life than those around him. In chapter 18, Abraham persists in requesting that God spare the two cities. Almost humorously, he asks God to save Sodom from pending wrath in the event that fifty righteous people can be found living there. But correcting himself each time, Abraham asks the same thing again and again—if there are just forty, then thirty, then twenty, and finally asking if there are only ten righteous people, will God save the city? God answers each time in the affirmative. Surely Abraham must have thought, in addition to Lot and his family, there must be a few other righteous people in Sodom.

After Abraham's time with God, the two angels who had been with Abraham earlier arrived in Sodom to find Lot sitting at the city's entranceway. After bowing to them, Lot insisted they come to his home. The angels hesitated, perhaps questioning Lot's heart, but then agreed to go with him to his house. Then we begin to see God answering Abraham's request. While at Lot's home, perverted neighbors come and want to have sex with the newly arrived angels. These misguided neighbors did not know the angels were from God, which was a mistake. Lot steps outside to speak with them, and even offers up his daughters to the neighbors! (He does this out of respect for his visitors.) The conversation goes poorly, so the angels pull Lot back into the house (19:10).

A few moments later, we find Lot unsure of himself, torn between listening to the angels as they say they are going to destroy Sodom and listening to his future sons-in-law laughing about the pending doom. Twice the angels tell Lot to hurry and take his wife and daughters out of the city—but Lot is indecisive. The angels show Lot great mercy, grabbing him (a second time!) and his wife and daughters to quickly get them out of the city. Escaping just in time, they safely leave Sodom before the destruction begins. If not for Abraham's repeated requests to God, would the angels have been so quick to physically grab Lot—twice—to save him and his family? There's a bit more from this story.

> *So when God destroyed the cities of the plain, he remembered Abraham, and he brought Lot out of the catastrophe that overthrew the cities where Lot had lived* (Genesis 19:29).

God answered Abraham, and God answers us today.

There is a lesson in Lot's reaction as well. If he could have seen into the future, if he had been able to see how it would all turn out in the next few moments—the destruction of Sodom, perverted neighbors wiped away, his very home abolished—do you think he would have hesitated? No! But note that it was *Abraham's* request, not Lot's. When we pray, we need to keep our eyes open and our hearts available for God's answers. Sometimes God makes answers to prayers obvious, just as the angels did for Lot. If we are not in tune with God's will, if we are not listening to Him, if we are not in prayer, we may not see answered prayers.

When it comes to your dreams, your goals to launch your life, you must have an impactful prayer life so your goals are His goals as well. Impactful prayers are full of worship, praise, and gratitude. They offer vulnerability and confession. Impactful prayers lend themselves to perspective around the sovereignty and will of the Father. Finally, they include confession and requests as well. If these things are not a priority for us, as they were not with Lot, we will find ourselves naively putting our confidence in the refuge of our own life and the security of our ways instead of in God's ways and will. It can also leave us quite indecisive during times when the right direction should be clear. Let's learn from Lot to stay close to God, His Word, and in prayer so we will have full confidence in God and the foundation we need in times of crisis.

Let's go back to David and Saul. There are many amazing lessons found in the precarious relationship between these two men that we can link to a great prayer life. While Saul was still the reigning king of Israel, God chose David as next anointed king. This decision didn't work for Saul. And throughout the long period of David waiting while Saul was king, we read the prayers of David in the book of Psalms and see his thoughts as he expresses them to God. And perhaps like our prayers, we see a wide range of tone and emotions from David. We see anger, frustration, resolve—and yet trust in the Lord as well, to name a few. One such psalm is Psalm 59, which correlates with a story we find in 1 Samuel 18–19. Here we find that Saul learns his daughter Michal is in love with David. Saul sees this as an opportunity to entrap David so he can take his life. Later, David and Michal learn that Saul is arranging to have his men secretly kill David while at home. With the help of Michal, David escapes out the window, surviving this unwarranted attempt on his life. David's emotions speak in Psalm 59 as he reflects on his thoughts during this time. He starts by asking for God's protection and, continuing in verse 4, acknowledges the injustice he feels in this moment. David says, "I have done no wrong, yet they are ready to attack me." His emotions range from fear, anger, and being overwhelmed with the injustice to trust, surrender, relying on God, and even rejoicing. David almost seems angry when he starts calling Saul and his men "evildoers" and "bloodthirsty men." During his prayer, he moves to acknowledge God's authority, and, by the end, he finishes with this: "O my Strength, I sing praise to you; you, O God, are my fortress, my loving God."

It is a remarkable look at David's transition in feelings and in his heart, all through his deep prayer life. We see his thoughts, his emotions, and his spirit turn to God. In wrongful situations, he finds his peace and security in the Rock. Now draw a parallel back to the persistent widow story Jesus told in Luke 18. Of all the circumstances Jesus could have used to illustrate the need for persistence in prayer, he chooses injustice. He doesn't choose financial difficulty, sickness, grieving, or any number of other challenging circumstances that require persistent prayer. Ironically, injustice is one of those things in which we can feel so "right" to be mad, bitter, and resentful.

All of us have endured hard things in our lives, including wrongdoings, injustice, or difficult emotional circumstances that require extra effort in faith, love, and persistent prayer. But, as usual, God inspires us. We've just discussed David's going to God in prayer during these times. We see this same persevering lesson at other times with David and throughout God's Word. In the book of Acts, we see Peter in prison in chapter 12; in chapter 16, it is Paul and Silas in chains. In 1 Samuel 1 we see Hannah persisting in prayer for years when she had to endure grief from Peninnah. In each of these occurrences, none of these people had done anything wrong. They were merely in hard situations, ones of injustice, of others wronging them, just like the persistent widow. Each time we see them praying, persevering, and being persistent—not complaining, grumbling, or giving up. They were prayerful when things were unfair. Their ongoing times with God gave them a foundation so that, in the hardest or worst situations, they knew God would be with them. Despite not knowing how their ordeals would end, they knew God was their strength, and they put their faith and trust in Him. They serve as prime examples for us during times when difficult hurts and injustices can sap our zeal for God if we don't pray and persist like these biblical heroes. It is impossible to dream for God if we are caught up in bitterness because of injustice.

Our reliance on God is reflected in our time with God. Is it a lifestyle? And is there a limit? Paul writes in 1 Thessalonians 5:17 to pray continually. We should pray about everything! It is exhilarating to walk outside and think about all the things you see, the air you breathe, the people you walk past—and to praise God for all of it! To consider His creation of the mountains and valleys, the earth and the heavens, the moon and the stars, the oceans, rivers, and lakes, the land animals, sea animals, and animals that fly—and all the details wrapped up in all these creations. They provide an endless trail of praise! It is miraculous how the full creation works together as one remarkable concert. God has moved, and still moves, in ways you do not know, all to support you. Perhaps even this book will be cause for a resurgent prayer life because you love Him, and He loves you desperately. We should humble ourselves and confess our shortcomings and sins to God in our prayers. He does not have to pardon us of our iniquities, yet He does.

Acknowledge how you have sinned against Him and perhaps

against others. Remind yourself that you will *always* fall short of God's glory and that it is He who loved you first. Be grateful in prayer, and spend time just thanking God for all He has done. Be thankful for all you see, the ways you see God at work, and grateful even for the ways you do *not* see clearly but still can trust that God is there. Be grateful for the changed lives of the people you love, the victories over sin, and the saved souls.

Finally, we all need prayers. Pray for those closest to you. What is it that they are working on in their character; what is going on in their lives? Even though Lot was confused at the moment, not in sync with the angels before him, Abraham's time with God saved him! Pray for others around you, coworkers, fellow brothers and sisters in Christ, your parents, your church leaders, leaders of countries—the list is endless. Pray for those in need, the poor, the hungry, the homeless. And pray for the gospel to continue to spread, for those studying the Bible for the first time, or for those who have left Christ. God answers prayer. No one has ever jokingly said at a funeral, "That guy prayed too much." There is no limit. When considering your foundation formula, there is no greater ingredient than praying to our gracious God. Let's take the time, get down on our knees, and be people of prayer.

BIBLE STUDY

If you celebrated Christmas as a young kid, you probably have fond memories of great food, decorating, and opening gifts that lay under the tree. At the Bruns' house, the stockings and tree would all be put in place several weeks ahead of the big day in anticipation of just the right moments. We have homemade decorations highlighted throughout our home. You can find a third-grade art assignment hanging on the tree, a first-grade "happy church" craft project set on a table, and a babysitter night holiday craft hanging on the wall, all in the effort to make the season bright. When decorating the house, everyone pitches in where they can. Decorating the tree is always the highlight of our holiday preparation.

But apart from the tree, the highlight of the season was and is the opening of gifts. When one child would be in that enchanted moment of first discovering the wrapped presents under the tree, a shout to all the others would lead to spreading joy. The colors, the surprise, the oddly shaped boxes and bags—all of it contributed to our young children gleaming with excitement. Gifts would be opened one at a time out of respect for each other. Every time a gift would begin to be unwrapped, all eyes would go to that gift and that child. Most times, all the children would gather around the one sibling who was opening a gift. As the gift would erupt from the wrappings and come into plain sight, there would be a joyful shout, wide eyes, big smiles, and maybe even some dancing! Opening gifts has always been a magical moment in our family.

God has given you a tremendous gift in His words. The Bible is a gift that continually gives, and it's the second ingredient in our foundation formula. We can open it every day with an eager expectation of learning something new, considering a more profound thought, or committing something new to memory. The Old Testament has stories of faith, bravery, and perseverance through God's endless covenant of love in forecasting the life of Jesus. We also read New Testament stories of great faith in Jesus, the power of the gospel, and how the gospel spread throughout the known world.

Everyone has a favorite Bible character, but these people are much more than mere individuals, and the Bible is more than a mere book. Sometimes, remembering the people in the Bible were folks just like us helps the words jump off the pages and come alive. These were people who lived, walked, and breathed. The men and women we read about in Scripture made mistakes, got angry, and had to go to sleep each night just as we do. They got grumpy on their bad days and shouted for joy when their lives were blessed. Have you ever imagined what the twelve disciples discussed with their wives and families the evening after they watched a herd of pigs run off a cliff? What did it look like when the shepherds saw the angels singing in the night sky? How would *you* have responded? Imagine what it must have been like to load the donkeys and begin walking with Abraham not knowing where he was going. Would you leave everything if you were in his situation? Envision the faith and transformation in Peter as he stood before thousands to tell the story of how their sins crucified Jesus. Was he scared? Would you have been afraid? Picture the humbling, bright-light moment when Saul talked with Jesus by himself—and soon after became Paul. Are you willing to make a crazy change like that?

The people in the Bible are inspirational, motivating, and they lived as examples to move our faith today. Their stories are there to impact our days, give substance to our lives, and spur us to greater heights in our faith. Their written accounts come to life so we may believe in this man Jesus, that He is the son of God and the Messiah. The descriptions are there for us to internalize, visualize, and imitate, not to gloss over. We don't need to know the type of fruit Adam and Eve picked, only that they each took a bite. What kind of large fish swallowed Jonah doesn't really matter, just the fact that he survived to teach about God, at God's direction, in the wicked city of Nineveh. Jesus' life should inspire us and build our confidence that, through Him, we have all we need.

> *I seek you with all my heart; do not let me stray from your commands. I have hidden your word in my heart that I might not sin against you. Praise be to you, O Lord; teach me your decrees. With my lips I recount all the laws that come from your mouth. I rejoice in following your statutes as one rejoices in great riches. I meditate on your precepts and consider your ways. I delight in your decrees; I will not neglect your word* (Psalm 119:10-16).

These verses were written by an author who was passionately devoted to God's Word, and that passion is evident throughout all of Psalm 119. The importance, the eagerness, and the profound longing are there, clear for the reader to see. It begs a question: is this your heart? Do you have excitement for God's Word that rivals a young child's Christmas enthusiasm opening his or her gifts? Is there eagerness in your heart to dwell on His ways? Do you think about His words at night? What do your actions tell you?

God intends for us to engage in His Word as the treasure that it is, but time can do odd things to all of us. As we age and become increasingly more familiar with the biblical stories, we can arrive at a place where we are distracted, uninspired, and our time with God lags. Reading the familiar story of David defeating Goliath can turn into only mildly encouraging words instead of deep inspiration from God that once again stirs the heart.

God knows us. He knows our weaknesses. In His mercy He offers His Word to us. God's gift is meant to be pondered, trusted, leaned upon, and remembered. His words are intended to direct us, give us answers, and bring us peace. Consider:

> *My soul is consumed with longing for your laws at all times* (Psalm 119:20)
>
> *Your statues are my delight; they are my counselors* (Psalm 119:24).
>
> *Direct me in the path of your commands, for there I will find delight* (Psalm 119:35).
>
> *I will speak of your statutes before kings and will not be put to shame, for I delight in your commands because I love them* (Psalm 119:46, 47).
>
> *I have considered my ways and have turned my steps to your statutes* (Psalm 119:59).
>
> *Your word, O Lord, is eternal; it stands firm in the heavens* (Psalm 119:89).
>
> *Your word is a lamp to my feet and a light for my path* (Psalm 119:105).
>
> *Because I love your commands more than gold, more than pure gold, and because I consider all your precepts right, I hate every wrong path. Your statues are wonderful, therefore I obey them* (Psalm 119:127-129).
>
> *Great peace have they who love your law, and nothing can make them stumble* (Psalm 119:165).

It's crucial to see the ongoing need for God's living and active Word in your life, to see the impact it can have, and to keep it as an anchor in your daily living. There are countless great books about God and spiritual principals, but none of them can—nor should they—replace God's Word and our time in Bible study. Which verse above is your favorite? Which one calls to you the most and why?

By tying impactful Bible study to the first ingredient, prayer, you will move closer and closer to a dependent relationship with God. God will bless a hungry heart, and He badly wants us to better understand Him and His words. Pray for wisdom and understanding that only God can provide, and pray that your deepening time with God can be reflected to those around just you as the moon reflects the sun on a clear night.

To underscore the need for your desire for God's Word, consider an Olympic athlete. Whatever their event, their skill was not something they picked up the weekend before by watching a YouTube video! They underwent strenuous training and gained a strong spirit that carried them. Think about that kind of effort for a moment—and then consider if your Bible study has that type of intention, focus, and desire. Don't just read the Scriptures and find them interesting, let them come alive in you! Help others see how this is true for you. Tell them what you are learning, how it is changing you, how it continues to stay fresh for you.

> *My son, if you accept my words and store up my commands within you, turning your ear to wisdom and applying your heart to understanding, and if you call out for insight and cry aloud for understanding, and if you look for it as for silver and search for it as for hidden treasure, then you will understand the fear of the Lord and find the knowledge of God. For the Lord gives wisdom, and from his mouth come knowledge and understanding. He holds victory in store for the upright, he is a shield to those whose walk is blameless, for he guards the course of the just and protects the way of his faithful ones* (Proverbs 2:1-8).

Consider all the ways you can to launch a deeper, more reliant prayer time and inspirational times in God's Word, the first two ingredients of our foundation formula. These two things will fuel your dreams for God.

PERSONAL MINISTRY

Mackinac Island, Michigan, is a favorite for thousands of travelers each summer; our family has been among them. It lies beautiful and serene in a picturesque setting in the northern Great Lakes. Set in the waters of the Straits of Mackinac, where Lake Huron and Lake Michigan merge, Mackinac Island is where you can see both the lower and upper peninsulas of Michigan as well as the Mackinac Bridge, an engineering marvel that connects the two points. The summer sunsets are spectacular, the colorful sky reflecting beautifully off the water on a clear, still evening. The crisp blue waters in the area are clear and provide cool refreshment should one dare to swim. On the island there is a small landing strip for smaller planes to land. Most visitors take a ferry over the waters; they hope for a smooth crossing on the Straits of Mackinac. On the ride over, the bridge lies portside and spans a five-mile distance across those beautiful waters. Upon arrival at the island dock, visitors find a quaint little town with a variety of shops, restaurants, churches, cottages, and the sounds of seagulls. The several fudge shops are extremely popular; they always have a line. Most visitors come to spend the day visiting the town and the rest of the area, but they don't ferry their cars. Bicycles and horses are the only two modes of transportation to navigate the island; the town is a walkable distance from one end to the other. There are a few roads and several spectacular views of the waters that surround the island. There is a natural rock bridge to visit and an old fort that has daily historical reenactments during the summer months.

Facing to the south, the Grand Hotel adorns the island hillside. Erected in the late nineteenth century, it is only a few stories tall but is very, very long. On the front of the building the world's largest porch extends the full length and height of the building. This eye-catching marvel of a porch has a light gray deck adorned with dozens of white rocking chairs. The hotel is nearly all white and has many windows and masses of colorful flowers nearby. The round pillars on the porch are impressively large and echoed by the rounded ends of the porch itself. On the street that runs before the building, horses and carriages move about transferring passengers to and from the hotel. It is all quite stunning and takes you back to another time! In front of the Grand Hotel is a large, lush lawn that extends the length of the building. It heads downhill toward the waters, where there are cottages, trees, and the rocky edge of the island. From the porch rocking chairs, one can see over the trees and coastline for miles, over the waters, the passing ships, the bridge, and to other parts of Michigan beyond. Visitors sit on the porch enjoying the cool breeze from the Straits and forget their troubles, if just for a time.

At night, while standing on the shore back on the mainland, you can easily see the beautiful colored lights on the bridge reflected on the Straits of Mackinac waters. Farther away, in the distance, you can also see the lights on Mackinac Island. While there are lights here and there, only one set of lights is clear as to its identity: the hotel. In the evening, the Grand Hotel lighting shines across the long white porch from end to end. From miles away, you can look across the Straits, the island shoreline, over the trees, and up the expansive lawn to the uniquely beautiful porch with rounded ends. The hotel is unmistakable. It shines like a beacon, like a town on a hill or a lamp on a stand. It's a picture of the third ingredient of our foundation formula: personal ministry.

> *"Neither do people light a lamp and put it under a bowl. Instead they put it on its stand, and it gives light to everyone in the house"* (Matthew 5:15).

> *"Now that the Lord your God has given your brothers rest as he promised, return to your homes in the land that Moses the servant of the Lord gave you on the other side of the Jordan. But be very careful to keep the commandment and the law that Moses the servant of the Lord gave you: to love the Lord your God, to walk in all*

> *his ways, to obey his commands, to hold fast to him and to serve him with all your heart and all your soul"* (Joshua 22:4, 5).

God intends for us to be a bright light. That light comes from our love and devotion to the Lord our God. Consider the Israelites after they crossed the Jordan River to the land promised them by God. Joshua probably knew the temptation that would soon come upon them, so he reminded the people to be careful, to love, to obey, and to walk with and serve God with all their hearts.

This reminder holds just as true for us today. If you're a Christian, you probably go to church regularly and may attend other services and activities through the week as well. Church activities exist for us to be encouraged, to see friends, to sing songs, and to worship, but they are not enough to fulfill the call to be a light on a stand. We live in a lost world that has endless needs. God has called us to a lifestyle that echoes the life of Jesus—and Jesus spent much of His life ministering to sinners, the sick, and the poor. His time with His "church," or disciples, was often spent in the environment of sinners, the sick, and the needy. And just like Jesus, we must have the lost and the needy on our hearts, spurring us to specific actions and a specific lifestyle. We need to have a personal ministry, a ministry in which we are actively reaching out to and giving to others.

Jesus reached out to many in His life, but whether the thief on the cross had seen Him before his final moments is not known. He certainly believed in God and knew something about God's kingdom, but, more importantly, he was confident in Jesus being the Son of God. This criminal would be the last person Jesus would reach out to in His personal ministry as He hung, dying, on the cross.

> *Then he said, "Jesus, remember me when you come into your kingdom." Jesus answered him, "I tell you the truth, today you will be with me in paradise"* (Luke 23:42, 43).

The agony Jesus went through is difficult to imagine considering the physical beatings on His body and back, the nails in His hands and feet, the blood loss, and the crown of thorns on His head. Beyond all that, most of His closest friends had deserted Him, leaving Him to face this battle alone. One of His best friends callously betrayed Him, and another had gone against his own words and denied that he even knew Jesus—not just once, but on three different occasions. At the start of this ordeal, Jesus prayed a long and difficult prayer to surrender His will because that was what He needed. It was the only way He would get through it.

For most of us, the closest thing to a crown of thorns that we have experienced is getting our pant leg caught on a rose bush. We have probably been hurt emotionally, however, by people close to us, and maybe even hurt physically. In the hours preceding, and in this moment, Jesus experienced the worst of humanity. It would have been painful for anyone. Corrupt people lied about Him and orchestrated His death. His followers and others He had taught were disloyal to Him and rejected Him. The guards put a horrible thrashing on His body while the religious leaders of the day stood by and gave approval. It was an ugly scene.

Nearing the end of this terrible ordeal, Jesus finds it in Himself to reach out to a neighbor, to make one last effort to help another person. It must have been quite a conversation to witness between Jesus and the thief! If you had been with Jesus before, you would have seen this kind of thing, and probably many times. The broken criminal knew something about Jesus and humbly came to Him in need. Jesus, in complete agony, verbally reached out to him, offering to be with him in paradise. Had His hands been free, Jesus, like so many other times in the gospels, would have looked him in the eyes, maybe held the man's hand or touched his cheek in encouragement and love. But all Jesus could give here were His words, and His words were enough. Those on the ground may well have heard the entire exchange. But what spoke loudest was Jesus' actions. Three nails, a crown, and emotional and physical beatings did not stop Jesus from loving this criminal, offering him hope in his last moments.

Our hearts and our actions should be inspired to turn to the outside world as well. What opportunities has God set before you? Are your eyes open? As you dream about your future, being a light in this world should be on your heart. The distractions, the waves, and the winds will always be there, and they can take your focus to something other than building a real foundation. However, if we are mindful of having a personal ministry, and if we go to God in prayer for those who need Him, doors will open. As Paul wrote to the church in Corinth, we are Christ's ambassadors, His representatives in this world. He wants us to be a shining light. He's there to help us be just that.

As always, however, the enemy is at work lying to you so he can stop you. At times, our fears and doubts keep personal ministry off our minds and hearts. Sometimes, it is merely our sinful selfishness or nonengagement that causes us to settle for being churchgoers. Our wayward efforts cause us to stop living as an example, or keep us from being the "go to" person at the office when someone is in need. Our times of prayer suffer, and we don't think about being a light in the neighborhood at a party someone is hosting. We stop being encouraging to our coworkers or classmates. We don't invest in purposeful friendships outside of our comfortable church friends. We become insular, and our shining light becomes focused on ourselves. We forget the very example Jesus set for us.

Having a personal ministry is much, much more than offering an invite for a Sunday service. It is being the lamp on the lampstand and living in a way that your neighbors and friends see you as a beacon of light. It is about having integrity in the workplace or keeping a godly attitude when someone else gets credit for your work. It is about having respectable character, about being the one who has a genuine concern for the coworker who has a sick mother or asking the classmate about their vacation. It is about being a hard worker, or an excellent employee, or a topnotch business owner, or being an honest example for others. It is about having God as your ultimate priority, about having your home or apartment an inviting haven so you can offer an invitation for dinner or maybe host a double date. And it is about the invitation to come and worship with you or to come to your home for a Bible study. Jesus saw the masses of people as helpless sheep. He saw the spiritual needs as well as the physical needs, and He offered Himself. Having a personal ministry is about love, encouragement, and offering hope. And when the time is right and God opens the door, you will be the help for the person who needs God, just like the criminal who turned to Jesus.

> *A man with leprosy came and knelt before him and said, "Lord, if you are willing, you can make me clean." Jesus reached out his hand and touched the man. "I am willing," he said. "Be clean!" Immediately he was cured of his leprosy* (Matthew 8:2, 3).

Even if you're a medical expert, you're not able to help with healing the way Jesus did. His medical practice involved, at times, shouting at a person, touching their hand, rubbing mud in their eyes, or some other creative healing technique. Rest assured, those with Him were always amazed at these moments, and the stories are fantastic for us to read. And while the lesson here is not how to heal someone physically, there is a lesson in being willing to give of yourself to those who have needs. There are always needs, whether spiritual, emotional, or physical.

The needs in this world are enormous. Every continent, every country, and every city has them. The elderly need care, the hungry need food, the young need education, and lost souls need salvation. It is daunting, intimidating, and frightening to consider the needs around the globe. We cannot meet them all. But where we can, we should provide support. Part of having a personal ministry is helping those in need around you, those God has placed in your path. The demands can come from people near us or in places we have never been, and sometimes they can hit our hearts very close to home.

As with prayer and Bible study, it is helpful to think intentionally about personal ministry. If you do, it will become visible to those around you. If you can voluntarily or financially support a charity, do that. If you can pass on the blessings God has graced to you, that ability is a great blessing. When Jairus came to Jesus (Luke 8) because his child was sick, he and his family had a great need. He asked Jesus to help his very sick daughter who was dying, and the Lord accommodated his request by going with him to see his daughter. Along the way, crowds were pressing against Jesus, people all around, and suddenly Jesus felt an individual touch Him in the midst of all these people. At the moment, Jairus was likely in a rush to get Jesus to his daughter's bedside. But Jesus took the time to find out who had *specifically* touched Him, and He subsequently made the time to meet the needs of another woman who was sick. What a lesson for Jairus and the crowd about meeting the needs right in front of you. Taking care of those in need was always a priority for Jesus and remains an example for us today. Jesus loved all people, and His ministry changed daily depending on the context in which He was ministering. Do your friends see this spirit in you?

If you have been in God's church for any length of time, your relationships have likely been the encouragement you needed in your darker days. Jesus calls us to love each other and have such obvious love that others will know we are His followers. That is a complicated task given that we are, in fact, human. We sometimes hurt each other, misunderstand each other, or have grievances of one sort or another against each other. Or sometimes we can grow extremely relaxed with our church family relationships and slowly stop relating to each other as an upward call to Christianity, giving way to making the church more of a fun-filled social club. These things work against God's will for us and work against the Scriptures that teach us to love one another deeply.

Finally, having a personal ministry is having friends and being a friend to people who are not in the church. In essence: be a light in the darkness. We see this in Jesus all the time. His followers wrote about the constant interactions that Jesus had with men and women who were not His disciples. He fed the five thousand. Crowds were with Him and pressed against Him regularly, and Jesus would often stop and notice the people and their needs. He knew at least some by name.

> *When Jesus reached the spot, he looked up and said to him, "Zacchaeus, come down immediately, I must stay at your house*

> *today." So he came down at once and welcomed him gladly. All the people saw this and began to mutter, "He has gone to be the guest of a sinner." But Zacchaeus stood up and said to the Lord, "Look Lord! Here and now I give half of my possessions to the poor, and if I have cheated anybody out of anything, I will pay back four times the amount." Jesus said to him, "Today salvation has come to this house, because this man, too, is a son of Abraham. For the Son of Man came to seek and to save what was lost"* (Luke 19:5-10).

Zacchaeus was a wealthy man but a man who had few friends. You may know the story, but did you notice that Jesus calls him by name before anything else happens? They knew each other before this moment. They had met, maybe had several conversations, but Zacchaeus's heart was not ready—until now. When he was ready, Jesus was there. And Jesus took a chance in their relationship by talking with Zacchaeus about some hard things he would need to change if he wanted salvation. As we see from Zacchaeus's reaction to Jesus calling him to repentance, the story has a great ending. Likewise, whether for longtime acquaintances or new friends, we need to have a personal ministry in which we serve as a light for them. Don't let your activities, work, or whatever the enemy puts in your path become a distraction or interference to your being a light. Make known the hope in your Christianity. Make it known so you can help others see it as well.

Take time to reflect on your personal ministry. This is something God wants us to pray about. It is imperative for our foundation that we build our life for God. If we don't plan or consider our impact, if we don't discuss it or pray about it, we won't be the light to the world we could be. Let's be real. It is too easy to rely on others to bring a guest to a worship service, and it's easy to let someone else be concerned with the folks in need. If you want to build a solid foundation, you be the one to meet needs. God has given you unique blessings, and you can reach out to people in ways no one else can. Who knows, maybe you will help meet needs in ways you haven't considered, or perhaps your friend is in search of spiritual help. Be the lamp on the stand, the city on the hill, the Grand Hotel on the Straits—be a shining light in a world that needs your help desperately.

Now you have the foundation formula! We will build on this foundation in the chapters to come. Faithful prayer, ongoing Bible study, and dynamic personal ministry give you a strong base on which to build your dreams. There are complete books written on each of the three ingredients, so we have been mostly brief on these topics. We are trying to focus these things alongside intentional living and decision making. While it can be a bit overwhelming, having intention in these areas will change your life and impact your friends as well. Talking with a friend or your spouse and working together to create goals can catapult you to the place of an inspirational example, creating great experiences for you and others. Put it to the test and commit these things to the Lord. You need a strong foundation to launch your life. You need a foundation that will keep you focused when the waves and winds begin blowing, trying to take your eyes away from the stronghold of your life with God.

PART II

You and Your Intention

Chapter Four

THE COMPLEX YOU

"Now then, just as the Lord promised, he has kept me alive for forty-five years since the time he said this to Moses, while Israel moved about the desert. So here I am today, eighty-five years old! I am still as strong today as the day Moses sent me out; I'm just as vigorous to go out to battle now as I was then. Now give me this hill country that the Lord promised me that day. You yourself heard then that the Anakites were there and their cities were large and fortified, but, the Lord helping me, I will drive them out just as he said." Then Joshua blessed Caleb son of Jephunneh and gave him Hebron as his inheritance. So Hebron has belonged to Caleb son of Jephunneh the Kenizzite ever since, because he followed the Lord, the God of Israel, wholeheartedly (Joshua 14:10-14).

This is an inspirational scene, an eighty-five-year-old man speaking in a powerful voice and leading the way in battle with all the younger know-it-alls! The other fellows with him may have been thinking to themselves: I want to be like that guy! As we discussed with the importance of our foundation formula in chapter three, Caleb's journey is yet another example. We can see his firm foundation of "wholeheartedly" following God.

In this passage, however, we see an additional insight into his thought process that led to this pivotal moment for the Israelites. Caleb, if even for just a short time, reflected on his life for the forty-five years he lived in the desert. With those four decades-plus in mind, he reasoned with Joshua about the hill county. Maybe he needed to convince Joshua or possibly reassure himself. Nonetheless, his zeal was contagious and convincing. Firmly asserting his age—or in spite of his age—Caleb based his request for the hill country on knowing himself better than anyone, knowing what he could do and what he wanted. He noted that he was just as strong as forty-five years earlier, and he had an infectious energy, one that led to the bold rallying cry of "give me this hill country!"

Just as his self-assessment gave Caleb confidence and a true forward motion, it is imperative for you to know your life and be grounded in who you are and what you want. Our first three chapters were about your dreams, your past, and your connection with God. Moving forward, you will be able to use this information to formulate an intentional direction for the next phase of your life. This chapter is about the complex you that God has created so amazingly well. You will have the opportunity to review how you spend your time and to consider your strengths and the opportunity areas that lay before you. This reflection will enable you to narrow your dreams to concrete thoughts that lead to specific actions that we will discuss in later chapters. As you read this chapter, you may find our *Action Planner* helpful as it has journaling prompts and templates for you to complete and help you discern choices for your future.

In considering the self-assessment concept further, think about other noteworthy or famous people in current or recent times who have had tremendous success in their fields. Consider how they lived and the deliberate actions they may have taken that catapulted them to be inspirational success stories. For example, Lebron James of the NBA has a passion for and extreme knowledge of the game of basketball. Mary Cassatt, the nineteenth-century American artist, had extraordinary expertise in painting. Cornelius Vanderbilt, a nineteenth-century American railroad tycoon, had a seemingly unparalleled understanding of business. Sacajawea, a nineteenth-century Native American, aided the success of explorers Lewis and Clark because of her deep understanding of Indian tribal culture, languages, and geography. Katherine Johnson, a brilliant African-American NASA employee, had a profound knowledge of math. And Washington Augustus Roebling, builder of the famed Brooklyn Bridge, had undeniable expertise in civil engineering. These noteworthy individuals were, or have been, exceptional at what they did in part because they liked what they did and developed a passion for it. Thorough knowledge, education, and training are prerequisites for outstanding achievement. But knowing yourself and what suits you to set your personal trajectory is no less essential. Recognizing your God-given talents, having a passion for using them, and using them so the world around you can be blessed will change the world.

Let's consider a short take on the life of Henry Ford. Ford was only 13 years old in 1876 when he first saw a motorized vehicle slowly rolling down a dirt road that had previously only seen horses and wagons. He had seen stationary steam engines before, but on this day, he observed that a neighboring Michigan farmer had creatively mounted a steam engine to a cart and connected a chain to the wheels, giving the cart the motorized ability to move. The makeshift machine was moving on its power, and the young Ford was inspired. He saw an opportunity and devoted his future to making vehicles. Learning how to launch this idea, however, wouldn't be easy. In addition to the challenges of creating a new product, there were plenty of other competitors working in the same space. Further, his work took much of his spare time and money. Ultimately, even as he built his first vehicle, he knew there would be very few customers. He knew that, initially, only the very wealthy would be able to afford an automobile. Despite these obstacles in front of him and many others, there was so much excitement for this new industry that more than three thousand automobile companies had formed in America by 1905! This, of course, included Ford's.

"I refuse to recognize that there are impossibilities. I cannot discover that anyone knows enough about anything on this earth definitely to say what is and what is not possible."
— Henry Ford

Henry Ford went to work, learning everything he could regarding the automobile. During many long evening hours in his shop, he engineered a full machine, often starting with a blank piece of paper. The entrepreneur cut each piece, turned every screw, and painstakingly mounted each part. In time he created his original version of the "horseless carriage" in a shed at his home. During the middle of the night of June 4, 1896, after forty-eight consecutive hours of finishing touches, the now undoubtedly exhausted Ford reached success. In a triumphant yet somewhat humorous conclusion, he had his first working automobile. Unfortunately, the door to the shed was too small to allow the new machine outside! So, after a bit of demolition work, Henry finally drove what he dubbed the Quadricycle out of the shed—at four in the morning.[5] It could not move in reverse. It had no brakes. It did not have a steering wheel. But Henry Ford was on his way.

In less than two years, Ford completed his second automobile, and then his third less than a year later, in 1899. The third had the ability to stop. In painstaking detail, each one of these early versions was an advancement on the previous design. Each machine was handmade, piece by piece. Every aspect was reviewed repeatedly by Ford, and where one part was wrong, he made a correct replacement. If it was wrong again, he repeated the process. Every system was developed from scratch, whether it was the steering system, brakes, axles, wheels, and so on. Ford knew every bit of his design and every piece that came together to create the new machine. He knew it all, inside and out.

It was this intense scrutiny and knowledge of each part that caused him to understand the vehicle so well. And it was through his work and design that he was able to envision a new way of producing a mass number of automobiles with a more cost-effective assembly line. The result was extremely successful; his detailed process made the automobile purchase affordable for many more consumers than merely the extremely wealthy. Henry's deep understanding of automobiles and his vision for assembly line production catapulted the Ford Motor Company to overwhelming numbers over the next few years. In staggering year by year increases, Ford sold 10,000 vehicles in 1908 and more than 18,000 in 1909. In 1910, there were 34,000 Ford automobiles purchased. This rate doubled in 1911, doubling again in 1912, all the way to nearly one half million autos sold in 1915! Amazingly, he sold almost one million automobiles in 1920, just twelve years after his first mass production year of 10,000 cars![6]

Just as Ford knew his vehicles and assembly line production, having a detailed knowledge of *yourself* dramatically increases your ability to launch your life successfully. Knowing what you like and dislike, what activities come naturally to you, and your challenges and passions—these are all critical in your ability to successfully move forward in the working world. In Part I, we discussed how God has prepared you, how He knitted you together and has grand plans for you. That is wonderful to consider, but unfortunately, God will not text His plans to you, nor will He tweet you the next steps in your personal development. He allows us free will. He will enable us to both fail and succeed. It is up to you to discover your inner desires and the things that make you tick. No one else can tell you what you like or dislike. That comes via self-reflection and self-discovery. To some, working through these waters comes easy. To others, it is indeed a difficult task putting all the pieces together, especially when you need to make a living at what you do!

In this chapter, we will unfold strategies to tackle this self-discovery so you can explore the complex and wonderful you. Even if you have a great idea of what you like or dislike, or what you want to do in your future, as you reflect on your past and see where your opportunities lie, you will be better able to plan for your future. God has made you to dream. We've discussed having dreams to do amazing things. Let's now explore *you* and how to start planning for the path toward that dream.

Hopefully, your reading, journaling, and the evaluation tools that we have provided in the companion *Action Planner* have set you up to be grounded in your dreams. Also, we trust that you see more clearly, through the first section of this book, how God has prepared you while you have a sense of how the enemy slows you down or inhibits your dreaming. Most importantly, we expect that you are incorporating the foundation formula in an increasingly and measurable way. We believe that intentional living comes from a deep connection with God and letting God lead you while you stay balanced in your view of your past, assess yourself in the present, and thus are able to make deliberate and concrete steps toward specific future goals. To that end, we've given you a few exercises to help with self-reflection.

In chapter two we discussed God's preparation of David, how one life event built on a prior incident, and then another, followed by another, clearly preparing David for God's use. If you haven't completed **Your History High Points** and **Your History Low Points** in chapter two of the *Action Planner*, it will help to take time to complete them now. If you don't have the *Action Planner,* take some time now to think back through your life and reflect on the formative highs and lows that shape who you are today. Think about the tasks that you liked and others you disliked. Think about the places, events, and people as well. What do they tell you about how God is preparing you or about who you are? What kinds of work, classes, and activities suit you or don't suit you? Take some time to journal and write this information down. It will be useful in shaping your goals.

In general, it is much easier to accept how God has blessed you in your high point moments. These are things like, say, either a good grade or an accomplished goal. We like to think about how God has blessed us through great moments, and we should. Don't underestimate the high points. Open your eyes to see how God has been at work for a long time.

However, it is essential to see and understand God's hand at work through low points as well. You've probably experienced low points that formed in you a resilient character that, perhaps, you have not internalized. Or maybe your difficulties have led you to a deeper understanding of the troubles that sometimes plague you. Trials and hardships can help us grow in compassion so we can minister to others. While we don't know exactly how he reacted in the first moments, David's confrontation with the bear was indeed trouble when it first came upon him. This is crucial: beyond just feeling grateful that he survived, he later viewed the moment of overcoming as a victory that he could speak to Saul. You have mastered many things that contribute to who you are today. So, look at your history in both the good and tough times to see how God has prepared you for what you are doing *right now*. Consider further journaling or discussion with a close friend to help you frame these events and challenges. In later chapters, we will see other biblical characters who had highs and lows as well, and we will see how God used those times as blessings later in their lives.

There is only so much time in your day. In chapter four of the *Action Planner*, there is an exercise called **Your Typical Week** to help you see how you're spending your time and what's working—or not. This activity in the *Action Planner* enables you to assess what parts of your life suit you in comparison to the ones that aren't working as well.

If you don't have the *Action Planner*, consider how much time you spend doing different activities during the week: work, time with family, chores, fun and relaxation, church, and more. In looking at your list of the things you do and where you spend your time, what do you notice? What motivates you? What would you like to change? What gives you energy? What frustrates you? Having a sense of your whole week will provide insight into what may be calling you for your future.

An evaluation of your typical week can be used to see your current state, the positive and the negative, in a way to help formulate your path forward. We don't want you to suddenly quit your job just because you don't like it—unless you have a solid plan to move your life ahead as a result. Don't think or act rashly. Life is a journey of many highs and lows. Through prayer, reflection, and godly advice let the insights you have now help you make choices to set a course toward a life that suits you better. Please use the evaluation process and assessment tools without shame—it's a time to recognize where and how you spend your time and energy so you can make changes to determine how those actions contribute or don't contribute to your ultimate goals. It's a time to learn about yourself, not beat yourself up.

Be aware of your enemy's traps and allowing your mind to wander to places it shouldn't. Think back to chapter one, in which we discussed ways the enemy deceives us. He would like nothing more than to twist your view of God and paralyze you into not moving forward. If feeling unsatisfied or unsure what to do, begin with what changes you can make in your relationship with God. Also, seek advice from those who can help you. Avoid the temptation to point fingers at others or circumstances. Choose instead to look at what solutions are within your sphere of influence or control.

If you have filled in **Your Typical Week** in chapter four of the *Action Planner*, you can easily see all the activities that take up your time. As discussed, you may have time allotted to a variety of activities such as work, school, or personal development. It's easy to think that the only parts that belong to God are the church meetings, Bible study group, or your own Bible study time. You may sometimes look at the other chunks of your week and see those as distractions from the "real time" with God. You probably don't see them as a spiritual time. That is not true! Does God care less of you during the time you're in class versus at a Sunday morning worship? Do you feel that God only truly cares about the 15 percent of your life used for either worship or some spiritual activity? Not at all. Our whole lives are in service of God (a good verse proving that true is Romans 12:1, 2). The fifteen hours of class a week and thirty hours of homework are in service of your relationship with God. Our forty-hour workweek, personal development time, and time spent encouraging our friends all have value in God's eyes. This concept may be new to you, but you will see this even more clearly in later chapters when we study other biblical characters. You will see how God used all the parts of our biblical heroes' lives in service of Him, similar to how we saw this with David.

In the business world, some companies choose to take part in what is commonly called a SWOT analysis. Although the origins are somewhat unknown, it has become a tool for many to assess, review, renew, or set a different direction for a company or work group. When a company takes on this assessment, a SWOT analysis reviews the current *strengths* of its organization, existing *weaknesses* of the same, viable *opportunities* that lie ahead, and the possible *threats* toward their future. This process is a perfect tool for self-reflection. There is a SWOT template in the *Action Planner* in chapter four. If you don't have the *Action Planner*, do some journaling of these concepts with the guidance given below.

S = Strengths

W = Weaknesses

O = Opportunities

T = Threats

God has woven unique strengths into your DNA; have you thought about them? Have you thought about what you have to offer the world around you? Sadly, it is easier to think about shortcomings and weaknesses. While we will look at those later, for right now, focus on your strengths. Dwell on these, and consider asking those close to you their thoughts. Think regarding what qualities and skills you can use and the ones you enjoy. For example, if you like being creative and are good at using those skills, that may be a space for you to consider professionally. What are the attributes that make you unique relative to others?

Honestly believing in and having confidence in being wonderfully created is a test of your faith in God. We looked at David taking on Goliath, but we did so from a bigger-picture view. Let's go a little deeper. David probably did not take time to stop and think about his strengths before his engagement with Goliath since this massive giant was taunting the entire Israelite army! David didn't pause to write a pro/con list deciding to shout or not shout at the giant or whether to take him on. In fact, from casual observation and the view of his fellow Israelites, he probably came across prideful, brash, and quite ignorant. But we know that attitude and confidence came from God and was a wake-up call to the spiritually sleeping Israelite army. It is with that same confidence that we encourage you to stand tall, look in the mirror, stick your chest out, and confess that you are a man or woman of God who has strengths and abilities to offer this world. Meditate on the things you like to do and do well. Again, ask those who know you best what strengths they see in you, and don't let the enemy lie to you. You have many gifts that are a unique combination found in no one else, so let's get them out there for all to see!

Conversely, in your self-analysis, you have weaknesses to consider as well. Before going further, please don't make this a moment of self-pity or allow this to stall your dreaming and planning. The enemy would love for you to dwell on your weaknesses for extra time, and he would be happy to over-emphasize their role in your life. You may conclude that you have a big stack of faults and a small stack of strengths. But while you have some of each, that conclusion would be a lie. As you consider the next step in launching your life, it is quite helpful to look at your whole package. There are areas where you need help or improvement. It's OK to admit this because it's good to know what they are to help focus your plans! Use your weaknesses to drive more clarity in your strengths. As an example, if you are introverted and consider your cold contact skills a fault, don't think about a sales career. Instead, consider leaning into a job that embraces introversion and your other strengths. Clarity, and focusing on your strengths while having an awareness of weaknesses, is a more productive way to move forward than thinking about fixing your weaknesses or dwelling on them too much.

You've considered your strengths and pondered your weaknesses.

Now take some time to explore opportunities that lie ahead. Where are there open doors in jobs or relationships that could lead to a better workplace for you? What career paths are hiring and can support you in full-time work? What open opportunities could you explore to see if they lead to a new job or profession that is a good match for you? This process can be fun, and you can even dream a bit. If you are graduating soon, or even in a few years, think about the opportunities in front of you. Do you have a job offer in your city or perhaps another state? Is there a company you could apply to that you have researched, that you believe is a good match for you? Go back to your strengths, and think deeply on the opportunities you might see in front of you. Be realistic and deliberate, but also perhaps stretch yourself a bit here. Where do you think God can take you?

Finally, be aware of the factors that can threaten your path toward opportunity. For instance, are you about to graduate but have a challenging class you feel will be difficult to pass? What do you need to do to ensure graduation? Are there financial considerations restricting your hopes for a possible opportunity? You have debt and need a job to sustain a lifestyle as well as pay off that debt. What careers can enable both? Perhaps the job market is closing in your field of interest in the area in which you live. How can you pivot your dreams? Consider your risks and the challenges ahead. Without a clear view of threats, we can make decisions that can cause career "headwind," cause harm, or ultimately set us back. So take the time needed to think clearly about these external factors that can derail your progress. Do not become overwhelmed by the threats; this is an opportunity to explore potential pitfalls, not get locked up in analysis paralysis. Remember to keep the strengths and opportunities in mind as you wisely assess risk.

We expect that taking the proper time to complete these three exercises will enhance your view of how God has been working throughout your life to provide you with a unique character and set of skills.

Your History High Points/Low Points: a better understanding of your past will give you a complete picture of how it can be used to inform your future.

Your Typical Week: having a strong grasp of your life and activities as you live them today will help you make course-adjusting choices now and in the future.

SWOT Analysis: Finally, an enhanced view of your areas of strengths against your weaknesses, and an assessment of your opportunities as well as threats, will not only encourage you to fly but give you a focus that points you where you want to soar.

Let's turn our attention to another biblical character who inspires us to soar because she fulfilled the life God gave her: the Proverbs 31 Woman.

> *"Many women do noble things, but you surpass them all." Charm is deceptive, and beauty is fleeting; but a woman who fears the Lord is to be praised. Give her the reward she has earned, and let her works bring her praise at the city gate* (Proverbs 31:29-31).

Whether you are a woman or a man, there is much to learn of the biblical personality who is known today as the Proverbs 31 Woman. Because there is a tangible description of her day-to-day life in just one chapter of God's Word, it seems worthy to take a detailed look at this woman's life. Obviously, from the Scripture above, her most noteworthy character trait is that she is "a woman who fears the Lord." Her humility is admirable, and she very clearly walks closely with God. A close study of this dynamic character can be both an inspiration and an example of the happiness and intention that can be found by searching and knowing your soul before God. Before going further, take a few minutes to read Proverbs 31:10-31.

This woman was married to a lucky guy! She had children who enjoyed seeing her each day! But the priority in her life was living in a manner pleasing to God (verses 29-31). She feared God (verse 30), regularly gave to those in need (v. 20), and while her body, like that of any person, needed rest, she did not let her spirit or life grow idle (v. 27). Think again about our foundation formula: her prayers would have been full of faith and humility as she grew in her fear of the Lord. Her study of God's Word would have been a regular priority since she spoke with wisdom and faithful instruction (v. 26). And her ministry would not have been just a simple invite to a Bible discussion group or church, but one testifying to her entire life, one she lived as an example for her children, relatives, friends, and coworkers. She trusted God when thinking of the days ahead (v. 25), choosing not to listen to the lies of her enemy nor to live in a state of worry.

Because of the apparent surrender of her spirit and life to God, she was happy. She filled out the life God gave her! Her story tells of a joyful woman who was all about God and was at peace in how He made her, and this joy reflected to the people around her. This strength of character enabled her to bring her husband good (v. 12) and to work with eager hands (v. 13). Her joy kept fear from controlling her (v. 21). And this left her husband and children saying nothing but great things about her (v. 28).

> *"The kingdom of heaven is like treasure hidden in a field. When a man found it, he hid it again, and then in his joy went and sold all he had and bought that field. Again, the kingdom of heaven is like a merchant looking for fine pearls. When he found one of great value, he went away and sold everything he had and bought it"* (Matthew 13:44-46).

The Proverbs 31 Woman's life matches the teaching we see here from Jesus. God and His people should be your most valued treasure. From that spirit and starting point you will be able to craft an effective life, a highly productive one, just as this woman lived. You will see yourself more clearly, know what you like and dislike, and see how God made you—extraordinarily so. You will not waste time regretting that you are not someone else, because you will be secure in who God has made you. You will trust God with your past and look forward to a promising future. You will trust your role in life, including your position at the workplace or how you serve in the church, and you will know that God values you. And your treasure with God will be a great motivator, just as it was for this woman.

Another character trait you can see in the Proverbs 31 Woman is how proactive she was. She did not sit back and let life come to her. She took it on. This famous chapter is filled with action verbs because that is how she approached her life and who she was through and through. She selects and works (v. 13) eagerly. She gets up early and provides for her family (v. 15). She considers, buys, and plants a vineyard (v. 16). She works and trades (vv. 17, 18) and makes coverings and linen garments to sell (vv. 22, 24). And, yes, she watches over her household (v. 27). She led her life by being alert and grasping hold of opportunity as it showed itself. She didn't miss opportunities by being blinded by distractions.

It is nearly overwhelming to consider the energy and intentional living in the life of this one woman. You may feel you can't begin to measure up to this woman in the slightest! Sometimes, however, we are only a few simple steps from being much more productive if we will take hold of a few concrete steps as we move forward. In considering how you spend your time, do you find regularly wasted time? Maybe you feel like you are spinning your wheels. Perhaps you are waiting for life to show up instead of taking it on. Many times, we do not need to look that far to see how we can be more productive or forward-focused. Often, a deliberate change to your daily rhythm can bring significant changes in productivity and forward focus. And purposefully embracing each task of your week can be a game changer. As an example, before or after church service is a great time to make appointments for the coming week to encourage friends in your ministry. Do you have an active plan to graduate, get a job, or grow in the position you currently hold? If not, make one. Advanced planning can help you be productive and happy just like the Proverbs 31 Woman.

Aside from her moments with God, she filled her time with working her job and taking care of her children and household. She is described as a wife of noble character (v. 10) because her entire life was in service of God. Letting that soak into your heart is essential. Too often, as previously mentioned, we separate the components of our life that we feel have nothing to do with God from what we consider the "spiritual parts." The Proverbs 31 Woman is a perfect example of why and how that is not true. She is an amazing woman who feared the Lord, and while her job was not her focus, she worked hard and earned money. She lives as an example for her children while caring for them, and she is deeply respectful of her husband. She is found in God's Word as a living example for men and women today.

In her SWOT analysis, her strengths were many, but perhaps among her weaknesses was her inability to know when to rest, or maybe she just wasn't a very good cook! But her hard work likely produced many opportunities for relationships. Praised at the city gate (v. 31), perhaps these relationships opened doors for her to be able to effectively reach out and share her faith in the Lord with many of her admirers. Her threats may have been something regarding her work, as can happen in any job.

Regardless of the weaknesses or threats, her shining character is one to be noted, and we will do well to think about applications from this woman to our lives. As you contemplate the complexity of your life—your strengths, opportunities, and future aspirations—how are you like her? How would Proverbs 31 read if it was about you?

Chapter Five

YOUR BRAND EQUITY

Whatever you do, work at it with all your heart, as working for the Lord, not for men, since you know that you will receive an inheritance from the Lord as a reward. It is the Lord Christ you are serving (Colossians 3:23, 24).

Congratulations! You've won a prize of five hundred dollars (let's pretend!) to use however you like. Where, and on what, will you spend it? Good shopping experiences you've had tell you there is searching, browsing, and then buying. So, what do you think you would buy? What vendor or store would you shop at to spend your prize money? If you're interested in items for your kitchen, would you go to Williams-Sonoma for lovely cookware? Or perhaps Target for style plus value? Maybe you would research online to be able to balance quality, recommendations, and price. Or maybe you have other ways to narrow your options for products and purchasing. What would make you choose one shopping experience over another? There are usually dozens of ways to purchase kitchen items.

How do your shopping decisions change if you consider clothing or entertainment?

Your perception of the product brand as well as the store or vendor brand will provide your answers.

Brands are everywhere. They each represent something; they call to us. If you stop and stand at a busy downtown street corner where there are cars and stores all around, you'll find yourself surrounded by branding. Each car and truck has a unique look and has branding on its front, back, and sides. You'll find that you covet some of those vehicles. But others? Not so much. You would also see a variety of stores, their signs in plain view. They may have big sale signs on the windows and brightly colored flags waving in the wind trying to grab your attention. You may be drawn to the Staples across the street because it has all the paper supplies you need. You may never so much as consider the convenience store next door because you perceive their sandwiches to be gross and expensive. You may see office structures boldly presenting the name of the occupant on the front door or at the top of the building. And, as people walk by, you see even more brands clamoring for your attention. You may see a man wearing Nike shoes carrying his McDonald's bag and a Coke, or a woman with a Gucci bag drinking her Starbucks, or three friends wearing their Old Navy gear playing on their iPhones, or a student with her North Face backpack checking her Fitbit. A Home Depot hat, an Adidas sweatshirt, a J.Crew jacket, or a Yankees T-shirt could all pass you by while you wait on that street corner.

Brands are everywhere, and they bring impressions and feelings whenever you see them.

Brands all vie for your attention and even cause a reaction on your part. For instance, which would you choose: Pepsi or Coke? Do you prefer Twitter, Snapchat, Facebook, or Instagram? Is it Starbucks or convenience store coffee when you are on the go? For clothing, would you choose H&M or Forever 21? Brands generally make you feel something good or bad. As we've talked with people on the simple topic of Coke versus Pepsi, some choose Pepsi because of taste while others select Coke because it's more available in local restaurants and is a bit more iconic. Not surprisingly, many prefer neither, and they might even find themselves a bit offended by having to choose one of these versus a more nutritional drink. They would rather have another beverage than accept either of these since the sugar and caffeine are so strong, and they don't feel right about drinking soda.

Social media branding causes huge reactions as well. What do you think about when you think of Twitter? How does it make you *feel*? That's right: how does it make you feel? Do you love Instagram and use it daily to post your latest photo? Do you look to Instagram to keep up with your friends? Does Facebook make you think about old people and distant relatives? Do you feel Snapchat is really for the very young? All these considerations are about branding.

Starbucks has thousands of stores around the world. We've seen them in Europe, South America, North America, Asia, and other places as well. When first founded, the chain's goal was to be the third home for its customers. That was the experience they set out to offer as a young, expanding brand. The first home is where you live, the second is where you work or go to school, and Starbucks wanted the third spot. Is Starbucks that for you? Is it the go-to place for you to have a conversation, read a book, or get a warm drink to get your morning started? Is it a place of comfort? Again, how does it make you *feel*? What do Starbucks, Nike, Rue21, McDonald's, and other brands stand for in your mind?

Believe it or not, like stores and products, people are brands too. For any person, their character is their brand. For example, did you have a "class clown" type in your high school? Is there someone at your work who is known as "the quiet one," or is there a "party animal" in your friend set? What people say and how they say it, how they act and carry themselves—all of this drives their brand. If you took the time to think about your coworkers, work group, or family in terms of familiar stores and shops, how would that look? Who would be The Home Depot guy who knows how to fix things? Who would be the Cabela's outdoor person? Who would be the Target, Panera, or Panda Express person in your friend group, and what does this say about them?

This exercise may be fun, but this book isn't about your family members or the people you know. It's about you. It is about your value to God, your dreams to soar and be used by God, and your making an intentional plan toward seeing those dreams come true. It is about growing in your faith and giving you a springboard to launch your life so you can be the best engineer, designer, public relations person, or medical person you can be. This is about you and the development of your brand.

And that is the brand called ________________________________. (Please write your name here and on the following empty spaces as you read.)

Have you ever thought about being a brand? What do you think the people around you would say about you, your character, or your brand? Think of it regarding brands you already know, both positive and negative. Let's say you are a Nike, General Electric, Sony, Apple. What makes those brands work, or not? What do you expect from your favorite brands, and why are they your favorite brands? If you shop on Amazon and love it, you likely expect to have your merchandise delivered quickly. You expect an easy shopping experience online, or you would likely shop elsewhere.

Now turn your attention to you. How do people experience you? Can people count on you to bring your best in whatever you do? What brand attributes describe you: honesty? integrity? being on time? hardworking? service-oriented? Or, with any of those things, are they not the case? After considering this, maybe for the first time, does the ________________________________ Brand (your name) need a branding makeover or upgrade? It's OK if you do! Sometimes even the biggest brands need a reset or an intentional plan for improving brand equity.

In the 1980s, Coca-Cola was the leading soft drink brand. At the same time, Pepsi was gaining ground through strong branding, product sampling, and effective ad campaigns. The Coca-Cola company chose to reformulate its almost one hundred-year-old formula to a slightly different taste to thwart the new competition. In April 1985 New Coke, as it was called, was placed on shelves everywhere, replacing original Coke. The new version was a disaster! Only 13 percent of soda drinkers liked the new formula. Consumers complained to Coca-Cola by the thousands. Many began to hoard what was left of the regular Coke as it disappeared on the shelves, stockpiling it in their homes! Coca-Cola executives discovered the Coke brand meant more than just flavor. It had history and emotion that connected the brand to the experience of drinking Coke. When shoppers opened a can of Coke, they were counting on the same familiar taste they had known all their lives. They expected the same emotional experience, but it was gone. The publicity in print and on television was so bad that Coca-Cola regrouped quickly to offer the old Coke on the shelves again, just three months after the launch of New Coke.[7] Eventually, New Coke would go away, the old Coke would stay, and it became known as the Coke Classic that is on the shelves in stores today. Sometimes, brands need a little work. In the same way, so do we.

The ______________________________ Brand takes deliberate effort on your part to grow into an attractive, desirable brand. Through God's Spirit, you have a chance to be a brand that people want to hire, reward, and develop. You have a chance to create the ______________________________ Brand in ways that can move you forward in life. You can be a brand that people will come to appreciate and desire as well.

At the beginning of this chapter, we shared a passage that Paul wrote in his letter to the Christians who lived in Colossae. It is a great Scripture to consider as you begin to think about the ______________________________ Brand. It highlights three keys, all found in verse 23, that can help you grow in your brand equity and allow you to increase in value in the workplace, class, or any current role in your life. As you consider your dreams, put a plan into action, and launch into your future, we strongly recommend you hold onto these principles. They can help your brand.

1) "Whatever you do . . ."

About a year before the writing of this book, our family was visiting the beautiful city of Hong Kong at the end of two intense weeks of traveling to several different cities throughout China. We were a bit tired, and we were strangers to this new city. It was lunchtime on our last full day of the trip. We had been on our feet for some time, and we were sure there would be a restaurant as we walked through the city. We were incorrect. The temptation to be crabby and impatient with one another was knocking at the door as we passed each city block not able to find food. Our feet were tired, and it seemed like all of Hong Kong was in our faces. We thought that, surely, after a few blocks, we would find a place to eat. After many blocks, lunchtime had passed, and now the regular hunger pangs turned into despairing cravings and longing for rest.

As we came upon yet another street corner, we spied an old familiar brand: McDonald's. It was so small that, had it been a garage, we were not sure we could have parked a car inside. Given the lack of other options, we chose to squeeze into the tiny restaurant and have our lunch there. While we did not discuss it at the time, we all knew what we would experience. McDonald's restaurants are the masters of having the same offerings at all their restaurants around the world. We have had McDonald's food in Cincinnati, Los Angeles, a host of other American cities, Shanghai, and now in Hong Kong. The cheeseburger, small fries, and Coke were satisfying, and they tasted the same as anywhere else we have been in the world.

Our brand—including our character, our faith, and our life—have a reflection regardless of what we do and where we are. Paul's encouragements to the Colossians are reminders that we can't just be Christians on Sunday mornings, at midweek church meetings, or when we are with our church friends. The passage is a reminder about having a consistent character from day to day, week to week, regardless of what we are doing. And to be intentional about who we want to be. Our love for God and obedience to Him should consume us and reflect in our daily lives. We can't have a good attitude when we are at church and unleash a different, worldly, self-seeking version of ourselves when we are with coworkers and classmates. What kind of brand would McDonald's be if it had different offerings, different looks, and different tastes from location to location? It's hard to fathom; wherever you enter a McDonald's, the cheeseburgers always look and taste the same. The ______________________________ Brand, its essential character, should be the same "whatever you do." There is no doubt that sometimes it is easier than others, but part-time Christianity is not the life that God desires for us. In fact, it is hypocritical and sinful.

2) " . . . work at it with all of your heart . . . "

There are so many great examples of men and women throughout history who gave their whole hearts to a cause that inspired masses. The signing of the Declaration of Independence in the summer of 1776 is one of these "all your heart" examples. One we still celebrate each July with impressive fireworks, backyard barbecues, and vacations to the lake. But to the fifty-six men who signed the original document, it was not a party or celebration. Not even close.

They were at the center of controversy. Some neighbors viewed them as rebels breaking from British rule; others considered them heroes. Of the fifty-six, fifty-four had families. All of them were outstanding in their communities, and they included doctors, lawyers, and many other professions. Ben Franklin was the oldest, at 70. Eighteen of them were less than 40, and three were still in their twenties. With the British looming nearby, the known risk for each of them was death by hanging for the treason of signing this declaration. They were principled and had sober minds, but most of all they were all in with all of their hearts.[8]

The British, of course, were quick to note the names of each man who signed. They responded with a targeted vengeance; they sought to find each man. As each signer was now on the run, several homes were burned—twelve, in fact, belonging to signers. Seventeen lost everything they owned. Many spent long chunks of time away from their families as they ran. But perhaps the man who gave the most was Abraham Clark. The New Jersey native had two sons captured and imprisoned on a British prison ship known for its brutality. More than eleven thousand jailed prisoners died during the Revolutionary War on this ship alone. Because they were the sons of a signer, the Clark boys received additional cruelty through starvation and harsh treatment. Finding Clark near the conclusion of the war, the British tried to bargain their ransom with him while his sons were still under their harsh brutality. The enemy offered Clark's sons' lives in return for a repentant heart, including a public expression of Clark's returned loyalty to the British king and Parliament. Given it was the end of the war, it would have been understandable for Clark to revert his loyalties, but he declined. He was all in with all of his heart, and at all costs.

In a later chapter we will discuss taking further action for your future. This Colossians passage is a significant and inspiring call from Paul for your present. Just as Jesus lived, we need to be all in, working at "whatever we do with all our hearts." If you are in the workforce, give all of your heart. This effort should not be dependent on how much you enjoy your job or how much credit you receive for the job you do. Such an effort should be a character trait. Consider that the enemy wants you to be halfhearted. He wants you to put conditions on your giving and hard work so that you hold back until it encourages you or brings you reward. Fight back; take Paul's words to heart. The ______________________________ Brand *can* work if you give it all your heart, whether at the job, in class, or serving the needy. The ______________________________ Brand *can* give your whole heart in whatever you do!

Giving your whole heart is actually a common concept in God's Word. Here is a small sampling of God's encouragement to us.

> *"Love the Lord your God with all your heart and with all your soul and with all your mind and with all your strength"* (Mark 12:30).

> *Trust in the Lord with all your heart and lean not on your own understanding; in all your ways acknowledge him, and he will make your paths straight* (Proverbs 3:5, 6).

"You will seek me and find me when you seek me with all your heart" (Jeremiah 29:13).

"The Lord commands you this day to follow these decrees and laws; carefully observe them with all your heart and with all your soul" (Deuteronomy 26:16).

"Even now," declares the Lord, "return to me with all your heart, with fasting and weeping and mourning" (Joel 2:12).

"Do not be afraid," Samuel replied. "You have done all this evil; yet do not turn away from the Lord, but serve the Lord with all your heart" (1 Samuel 12:20).

3) " . . . as working for the Lord . . . "

We are instructed to let Jesus be our motivation and the source for all our actions. We are to let Jesus drive our character and who we are from day to day. Paul states the key is to understand that whatever we do, we do it as if we are working directly for Jesus. If we are working, we report to Jesus. If we are in school, our professor is Jesus. If we are spending time with friends, it is for Jesus. If we are alone reading a book or away with family, we are doing it for Jesus. This motivator will produce the consistent ______________________________ Brand that we previously discussed. It is the one common theme that is the same regardless of what we are doing or what our day may bring us. If we are always working for the Lord, that will cause us to be the same person, with the same character and same brand, regardless of how we are spending our time.

Paul wrote not as though he was giving some far-off, out-of-touch instruction; he spoke from his own heart and experience. Just a few years before his letter to Colossae, he wrote about his motives in his second letter to the church in Corinth.

For Christ's love compels us, because we are convinced that one died for all, and therefore all died. And he died for all, that those who live should no longer live for themselves but for him who died for them and was raised again (2 Corinthians 5:14, 15).

These words are not a call to be extra religious, or to think about Jesus a little more than usual on Sundays. Go back to earlier chapters, remember how God has prepared you, and then ponder your foundation formula. Do you understand the immense love that God has for you? Do you feel that love? Do you understand and feel the immeasurable value God has placed on you through His actions at the cross? Is this motivating you to build a strong personal foundation as you begin to dream of soaring? In the world's eyes, your brand should be most greatly motivated by income or by doing what you like for selfish enjoyment. But in God's eyes, in whatever you do, the ______________________________ Brand works at it "with all your heart as if working for the Lord."

If your past has been affected by abuse, tragedy, or hardship, consider that we are all new creations in Christ (2 Corinthians 5:17). God wants to create in you more than just a brand; he wants to give you a new identity based on His words, not words you've heard from another person. He wants to provide you with a lasting character based on His gauge of worth, not the treatment someone else gave you out of their brokenness. It's important that, as adults, we recognize God is our ultimate parent; He is the one who guides and governs who we are from now forward. If you've experienced a hit to your self-esteem and confidence from words thrown at you, remember the only words that truly matter are the ones the Lord speaks to you. Your brand, your identity, are treasures to the Lord.

You don't have to walk this journey alone or without example. God's Word is incredibly applicable to your life today. Through hundreds of examples, the Bible helps in areas of career and future dreams. Examples also help us understand the concept of using our whole life in service to Him. You'll find that the notion of building a solid foundation by a deep, active walk with God and giving God all your heart is not just theoretical, it's a concept that leads to action. There are biblical characters who never spoke of their brand, and yet they had one. They had dreams to be used by God. Their efforts, and their whole hearts given to God, proved these dreams drove them.

The examples we will look at next are accounts of people who dreamed for God and were driven by the role or work God provided for them for His eternal purpose. These were people who strove for excellence in faith and soared on wings like eagles. They weren't aspiring to fame or wealth but merely desired to do God's will. Because of this, they all had great brands that we can emulate today. They are there for us to study. We can observe their faith, reasoning, actions, and intentions. Let's see how these men and women can inspire us today. If your past feels daunting to you in claiming your brand, take heart! See how many biblical heroes overcome significant obstacles and challenging histories to show us the way.

NEHEMIAH

> *When I heard these things, I sat down and wept. For some days I mourned and fasted and prayed before the God of heaven* (Nehemiah 1:4).

It was the 400s B.C., a time of political and social power struggle. The Assyrians and Babylonians rose to power, and the exiled nation of the Israelites was scattered. Kings warred against other kings to expand control over people and lands. There were renegade efforts to undermine kings that led to assassination plots in their own homes. As you might imagine, it was difficult for a king to trust those around him. Often, perpetrators poisoned kings through food or drink. (Although about a century later, Alexander the Great was a good example. He was stricken by a sickness that would lead to a slow death within two weeks. He was just 32 and already world-renowned. Most experts agree that a deliberately poisoned cup of wine caused his sickness that eventually led to his death.)

Because of this ever-looming threat, the cupbearer to the king was one of the most critical and trusted positions. The cupbearer was responsible for delivering a cup of non-tainted wine to the king. In many cases, he drank from it first to protect the king. It is within this context that we learn Nehemiah lived and worked as cupbearer to his king.

The rise of the Persian Empire following the Assyrians and Babylonians was a blessing of sorts to the Israelites. While the Assyrians and Babylonians uprooted the Israelites from their lands and destroyed their towns and way of life, the Persians were more about keeping harmony in politics, social networks, and religion. At one point, Cyrus king of Persia (Ezra 1) was moved in such a way by God that he let the Israelites return to Jerusalem to rebuild the city and restore the previously destroyed temple. Imagine the excitement in the Israelite community to hear such good news after six decades of captivity! Forty-two thousand people returned to Jerusalem, and Cyrus continued to help the effort by returning articles from the temple that the Babylonians had stolen years before. But given the cultural diversity of the time and the transient nature of exile, not everyone was helpful in the return and rebuilding of Jerusalem. Factions of opposition formed against the Israelites returning to Jerusalem.

Nehemiah's path to a high role in government is not known, yet we see much about his character, faith, and the Nehemiah Brand in the book that bears his name in the Bible. He was the cupbearer to Artaxerxes, the Persian king. He was an Israelite who surely rejoiced at the initial news of the return to Jerusalem. However, the news of the social climate and destruction of the protecting wall and its gates was too much for Nehemiah, and this news led to his troubled heart shown at the beginning of the book of Nehemiah. It is an example for us on several fronts. This wasn't just bad news; it was devastating. Many times, we hear of bad news, even news that may cause emotion, but it is only the exceedingly dreadful news that makes us sit down and weep as Nehemiah did. How did he respond? Did he get mad and lash out? Curse God? Not at all. Nehemiah turned to his foundation formula: he mourned and prayed and fasted for "some days." While it is not clear how long "some days" were, what is clear is that he turned to God for help with his sadness. We also learn throughout the book of Nehemiah about his relationship with King Artaxerxes and his work to rebuild the wall, and how his brand and character come shining through his efforts.

Nehemiah was extremely trustworthy, which is an extension of honesty and follow-through. Full of integrity, he was a person who did what he said he was going to do and finished it with excellence. He had to be an honorable soul to be the cupbearer and protect the king in such a faithful way. The king counted on him for his very life. But Nehemiah did not view this as a peer relationship. He admired the king and did not believe he was owed anything from him. Despite Nehemiah's reverence for his king, a very close relationship also developed. After his time of prayer, the king noticed the sadness in Nehemiah's spirit. It showed in his face. In Nehemiah 2, they have a heart-to-heart talk in which Nehemiah fearfully asks the king for time away to rebuild the wall. Instead of responding negatively—striking him down, or closing the door to his request in some way—the king supported Nehemiah's return to rebuild the wall. The king did not even question whether Nehemiah would return to Babylon upon the wall's completion.

Because of his honest character and trusted brand, both Nehemiah's ongoing success in the king's inner circle and the king's support for Nehemiah's cause came despite the two having significantly different religious beliefs.

> *Then I said to them, "You see the trouble we are in: Jerusalem lies in ruins, and its gates have been burned with fire. Come, let us rebuild the wall of Jerusalem, and we will no longer be in disgrace." I also told them about the gracious hand of my God upon me and what the king had said to me. They replied, "Let us start rebuilding." So, they began this good work* (Nehemiah 2:17, 18).

In Jerusalem, other people saw the ruins, the devastating damage to the city, and especially the damage to the wall. The city of Jerusalem was vulnerable, and the people were brokenhearted and worried. It is Nehemiah who stands in, envisioning the wall rebuilt. He had a clear view of the tall task ahead, and by his faith in God he was able to look past hurdles that came his way. Nehemiah calls the people to action, and they build. He knew God was with him, and he did not shy away from this huge task, nor did he give up when it became increasingly difficult.

There were problems along the way, and the job wasn't easy. There was rubble everywhere. The builders were mocked and became targets of disparaging plots as they began their work. There were potential problems on all fronts that could have sidetracked and discouraged Nehemiah. Further, as he continued with this massive project, the builders were understandably and increasingly fatigued. Pessimistic rumors were spreading. Still, somehow, Nehemiah's spirit sustained the laborers. His vision of completion moved the builders past the naysayers, and his skills helped protect them from those with evil intent. He wanted to get the job done regardless of the problems at hand, and, stone by stone, the wall took shape. In just fifty-two days, much faster than anyone imagined, the wall was completed.

Let's look again at our foundation formula. Nehemiah believed in the power of God. As the foundation of the wall took shape, it was his firm spiritual foundation that carried him through the wall's rebuilding. His spiritual foundation was a part of him. And while there is nothing written about his childhood, he must have seen how God prepared him for this moment. God opened the door for him to use his talents, even before a nonbelieving boss, the king of Persia. Nehemiah did not doubt, nor was he swayed by the multitude of obstacles. He used his knowledge and his conviction to do the work God put on his heart.

There is more to learn from this great man, and we encourage you to read the book of Nehemiah to discover more about his character. But from this short study we can see that, clearly, the Nehemiah Brand was reliable under challenging times. It was a brand that was responsible and trusted in a world of mistrust. And whether the king or God, Nehemiah approached authority with humility and reverence. The Nehemiah Brand was defined by a remarkably diligent work ethic despite surmounting difficulties and mayhem, and all of this to God's glory.

LYDIA

> *The Lord opened her heart to respond to Paul's message* (Acts 16:14).

In their continued quest to share the good news of Jesus, Paul and those with him left Troas and made their way across the Aegean Sea to what we now know as northern Greece. While bypassing a few cities, they settled about ten miles from the seacoast in the influential Roman city of Philippi and stayed there for some time. It was a city of wealth that was central to the gold-producing region in the Macedonian district of Rome. Sometime earlier, many Roman military leaders were given land in the area, so there was massive allegiance to Rome among the citizens and pride in who they were as well. Consequently, there were very few Jews in the area and thus no synagogue for worship for those who were there. Today, the city exists only as a ghost of past ruins, but lessons live on of a remarkable woman who lived there approximately 50 A.D. One day during that period of history, Paul left the outer gates of Philippi to head toward a secluded cove at the river to pray. God worked the timing so that Lydia, along with other women, beat Paul and the others to the riverbank.

Lydia was from Thyatira, another city of the past that sat in today's western Turkey, about fifty miles inland from the Aegean Sea. Because of its abundance of water sources, it was an area recognized for its dyes and the business of coloring cloth. Lydia, while possibly having dealt in other dyes, was especially noted as a dealer of purple cloth. The process for dying cloth purple or deep red was complicated. The formulated dye came from a combination of individual sea snails and salt, and the process took time. Purple dye required an immense number of harvested sea snails; the secretion from one would produce minimal coloring. Individual threads were dyed before woven into a cloth which was then subsequently made into robes and other articles of fine clothing. This method of working with lots of snails was laborious and thus led to costly fabrics that few could afford. Lydia was working in Philippi to sell such cloth when she met Paul at the riverbank.

It is possible Lydia was widowed; there is no mention of a husband. Regardless, what is certain is that God was working in her life preparing her for this moment. There is little doubt her customers and working associates would have been predominately male as she worked in the purple cloth industry, but this day she was with a group of women as Paul approached. Paul, and possibly others with him, reasoned with the group of women, explaining Jesus and the good news of the forgiveness of sins. There may have been questions asked, opinions shared, and thoughts provoked, but at the end of their time, Lydia answered with action. God, in His preparation of this woman, opened her heart to respond, and she was baptized to receive the forgiveness of her sins.

As it was with Nehemiah, there are characteristics of the Lydia Brand to take to heart today.

She was personable yet confident, driven, a fighter. We believe this to be true because working successfully as a dealer in a high-end industry like this would require these kinds of qualities. For women today, working in a male-dominated industry or field can be difficult and, at times, feel like an uphill climb. How a woman dresses, walks, and talks are all sometimes consciously or subconsciously scrutinized. There is no reason to think this would have been different for Lydia. She may have been propositioned from time to time, and perhaps she was ogled at times by clients or passersby. Others may have dismissed her opinions. Nonetheless, her drive and personality enabled her to look past the hardships she may have faced as she searched for the missing piece in her life. And then . . . through Paul and his companions she found a path to a relationship with God. Encouragingly, her confidence would come shining through shortly after her decision to be baptized. To Paul and those with him, this was her request.

> *"If you consider me a believer in the Lord," she said, "come and stay at my house." And she persuaded us* (Acts 16:15).

It took some convincing, but she persuaded Paul and the others to stay at her home. Lydia was an incredibly dynamic woman.

To many Christians today, she is noted for being hospitable, especially to Paul, as she made her compelling invitation. But her character went deeper than merely being a welcoming host. Lydia had a loving heart for people and, most importantly, a steadfast heart for God. We see this in two ways in the brief Bible passage in Acts 16:14, 15. While it is unclear how the moment unfolded, Lydia made sure her household also was part of this story. When she first heard the good news of Jesus from Paul, her concern was not just for herself but also for those who were closest to her. As a result, those in her household were baptized for the forgiveness of their sins as well. What a victorious day for those who were there! Second, it was out of her newfound love for Paul and the others that they received the special invitation to stay at her house. Paul loved this woman enough to share the hope of Christ and show her a saving relationship with God. He taught Lydia about her value in God's eyes, the effect of her sins on her life, and the hope that was hers through the cross and resurrection of Jesus. Paul loved her in a completely platonic way, in a way no one had before. She was grateful and responded in love to God by showing these new friends love by inviting them into her home.

In the book of Revelation, written decades later, we read about a church in the city of Thyatira, Lydia's hometown. While we see only a small glimpse of Lydia's life in Acts, it is hard to imagine she did not have some influence on the church in Thyatira as we read this description of the church's character as a whole.

> *"To the angel in the church of Thyatira write: These are the words of the Son of God, whose eyes are like blazing fire and whose feet are like burnished bronze. I know your deeds, your love and faith,*

your service and perseverance, and that you are now doing more than you did at first" (Revelation 2:18, 19).

Lydia's impact could be similarly described: "Lydia, I know your deeds, your love and faith, your service and perseverance, and that you are now doing more than you did at first." By using her life in service to God, Lydia the businesswoman had an impact far beyond what she would know.

The Lydia Brand is striking. Displaying her qualities of confidence and drive, deep convictions, humble response, and loving faithfulness will enhance any believer's life for the good, as well as provide a light for the world around you. God prepared Lydia just as He prepared you. She may have undergone hardships or challenging circumstances, but with God's help she took on a new identity in Christ and become a new creation. We believe she gained a newfound vision for herself by the river that day and started dreaming for the rest of her life. You can as well as you consider the ______________________________ Brand. With God your brand can be substantially more impactful than you might think.

DANIEL

"Praise be to the name of God forever and ever; wisdom and power are his. He changes times and seasons; he sets up kings and deposes them. He gives wisdom to the wise and knowledge to the discerning. He reveals deep and hidden things; he knows what lies in darkness, and light dwells with him. I thank and praise you, O God of my fathers: You have given me wisdom and power, you have made known to me what we asked of you, you have made known to us the dream of the king" (Daniel 2:20-23).

The book of Daniel is an incredible story of a young man who faced numerous peaks and valleys in his life and career. We encourage you to read the full text for more detail on the story, and this will allow you to draw useful conclusions. We will briefly summarize some highlights here, as well as offer thoughts on how you might find yourself more similar to Daniel than you might think.

A few decades before the time of Nehemiah, King Nebuchadnezzar rose to power and ruled in Babylon. He was the king who besieged the city of Jerusalem and stole the valued treasures from the Jewish temple. He exiled Jehoiakim, king of Judah, from Jerusalem. Nebuchadnezzar was ruthless and did not believe in gods he had not created. In his vicious attack on Jerusalem, he destroyed much of the city and took many Israelites from their homes to live as captives in Babylon; he left only the poorest behind. Continuing his cruelties, he ordered his chief of the court officials to single out some of the captured Israelites for duty as his servants. He required the chief to find young men who stood out from the rest, who demonstrated a high aptitude for learning, and who were handsome and seemingly without defect. The plan was to incorporate them into the new culture by learning the language and literature of the Babylonians. This brainwashing of sorts even included new names given to these young men. It would take three years of training before they would be accepted into service of the king. Among this group of young men chosen by the chief was a special young man named Daniel.

Daniel had three other friends chosen from Judah among those being trained, and they joined many others who qualified for the training. They learned the Babylonian culture and were instructed to eat food that differed from that of their culture. For centuries, God had given specific instruction to the Israelites on what foods were acceptable to eat, and the faithful followed these decrees, including Daniel. To stay true to his faith, Daniel asked the guard whom the Babylonian chief official had placed over him if he could *not* eat the food the king offered. Perhaps this request risked his very life. Daniel asked for a trial period of eating only fruits and vegetables. After passing this trial period, Daniel and his three friends were allowed to eat the foods that aligned with their faith.

But God wasn't done preparing Daniel for what was to come.

To these four young men, God gave knowledge and understanding of all kinds of literature and learning. And Daniel could understand visions and dreams of all kinds (Daniel 1:17).

Despite the difficulties of his youth—including the loss of country, culture, freedom, language, family, and name—God continued to equip Daniel, and this young man grew in resiliency, wisdom, and faith. At the end of his three years of training, Nebuchadnezzar had a sort of interview with Daniel, his three friends, and all the others who went through the Babylonian program. Daniel and his three friends won the job. Not only did the king keep the four young men in his service, he also noted them as being ten times better in wisdom and understanding than those already working for him!

Nebuchadnezzar was the world's most powerful ruler; a great deal of weight was upon him. Perhaps he had many troublesome nights of sleeping. He was having disturbing dreams, visions that the king's experienced employees were not able to explain. Due to this, and with fierce anger, he ordered the execution of all the wise men of Babylon, including Daniel and his three friends, who had not yet even had a chance to confer with the king about his dreams. But instead of fearing the impending doom or being mad at the God who "caused this injustice" in his workplace, Daniel chose to plead with God in prayer. He went back to his foundation.

God answered Daniel's prayer. The praise that Daniel offered to God in gratefulness is at the beginning of this section, from Daniel Chapter 2. Neither his early extreme difficulties nor his later successes distracted Daniel from his foundation in God. He kept his eyes on God, planted himself in his convictions, and let God use his entire life to His glory.

Daniel successfully explained the disturbing dreams to the king. Instead of a bloody execution, the king promoted Daniel to be ruler of Babylon and placed him over all the other wise men. His career was going extremely well, but Daniel was just at the beginning. The talent of interpreting dreams given him by God was astounding, and the king was delighted with Daniel's wisdom. Later, Daniel's unwavering belief in the true God and His good works seemed to win the king over, and Nebuchadnezzar became a believer himself.

> *"Now I, Nebuchadnezzar, praise and exalt and glorify the King of heaven, because everything he does is right and all his ways are just. And those who walk in pride he is able to humble"* (Daniel 4:37).

It wasn't a simple invite to believe in God that won the king over. Instead, the king saw the true God through Daniel's living example, excellent work, and deep convictions. The king saw something in Daniel's faith that he wanted as well. This recognition of Daniel's faith is surprising because of the brutality and heartache the king brought to Daniel's people through the conquest of Judah and its exile. Daniel's impact came entirely through his character and branding.

There were more difficult times ahead for Daniel, however, just as there are for most people. Further testing of the Daniel Brand would come when King Nebuchadnezzar was succeeded by another king, possibly his son. Challenges often occur when there are personnel changes in the workplace, church, or other groups in which you may be involved. When the old leaders leave and the new enter, the new guard generally wants to make its mark, and the ways of the past give way to a new future. Change is rarely easy.

The new king, Belshazzar, didn't know Daniel. When he experienced an event that terrified him, the king needed to be convinced about Daniel through a talk with the queen. While the new king had not known Daniel personally, he had an impression of Daniel's brand. Do you see the Daniel Brand that the new king saw?

> *So Daniel was brought before the king, and the king said to him, "Are you Daniel, one of the exiles my father the king brought from Judah? I have heard that the spirit of the gods is in you and that you have insight, intelligence and outstanding wisdom. The wise men and enchanters were brought before me to read this writing and tell me what it means, but they could not explain it. Now*

> *I have heard that you are able to give interpretations and solve difficult problems. If you can read this writing and tell me what it means, you will be clothed in purple and have a gold chain placed around your neck, and you will be made the third highest ruler in the kingdom*" (Daniel 5:13-16).

At this moment, Daniel's career was once again on the line. Success would bring rewards, but failure would reap severe consequences given the queen's recommendation of him. Daniel, feet planted firmly in his foundation, explained the writing to the king's satisfaction. Again he was victorious and proclaimed third highest ruler in the kingdom. Unfortunately, only hours later, Belshazzar would be slain, and a new king would take over. It was yet another change.

King Darius was now the ruler, and he appointed Daniel, along with two others, to oversee 120 subordinate rulers throughout the land. As we would expect, Daniel was exceptional in his role, but this led to the irritation and jealousy of the other rulers. This time, not all things were working in Daniel's favor; there was severe corruption in the leadership group. Daniel was probably exposed to deceit many times and very possibly encouraged to join the lies.

> *At this, the administrators and the satraps tried to find grounds for charges against Daniel in his conduct of government affairs, but they were unable to do so. They could find no corruption in him because he was trustworthy and neither corrupt nor negligent. Finally these men said, "We will never find any basis for charges against this man Daniel unless it has something to do with the law of his God*" (Daniel 6:4, 5).

Wherever there are people, there is always potential for wrongdoing. Daniel's situation was no exception. As he stood alone in righteousness, others worked together to lie and manipulate the king's view of Daniel. They set him up and then spied on him in the hope of removing him from his new position.

When things go well, or if they go badly—in either case—we always need our foundation formula. In this case, after being manipulated by corrupt men, King Darius issued a decree that for thirty days no one could pray to anyone except himself or face certain death in a den of hungry lions. This presented Daniel with yet another life-defining decision. Daniel could have chosen to wait to pray for thirty days. It was not that long, especially given the life-threatening circumstances. He also could have simply prayed less, or prayed quietly to himself, in total isolation, while this law was in place. He could have taken many compromising actions to stay in the clear for just four short weeks. Indeed, he may have been tempted to think that God would understand. But Daniel reasoned differently.

> *Now when Daniel learned about the published decree, he went home to his upstairs room where the windows opened toward Jerusalem. Three times a day he got down on his knees and prayed, giving thanks to his God, just as he had done before* (Daniel 6:10).

After Daniel was caught in prayer by those who set him up, the king reluctantly threw Daniel into a den of lions. His career with this group of nonbelievers was at a low point, and he faced complete injustice through no fault of his own. God was at work, however. For a full night, God caused the lions to do nothing more than look at Daniel, lick their chops, and maybe take a sniff or two. His life was miraculously spared. God transformed this low point into a dazzling victory for Daniel. Later, and not surprisingly, it is noted that Daniel prospered in his role during Darius's reign.

Let's take a few moments and reflect on Daniel's life in his early years. While there is no information written about him or his family before his time in captivity, we can easily imagine what life must have been like. The king of his faith had fallen. The Israelites were in spiritual disarray. He was taken captive from his home and native land. Likely, he was separated from others whom he loved, and now he was chosen to serve a nonbelieving king who had caused all this upheaval in his life. It would have been understandable for a young man in these circumstances to question his belief in the all-powerful God in whom he put his faith when he was young. It would have been easy for him to give up and be angry, or to succumb to the ways of the new land, giving up his faith altogether because he might have perceived that God had given up on him. The dark path of his youth might have taken his story in many wrong directions. But, as we've seen, Daniel was not one to give up and take the easy path. He never gave up on God.

We have discussed much about how God has prepared you for an impactful life and how, from the beginning, while still in your mother's womb, God was wonderfully at work. Hopefully, you have taken note of this in your personal life, in your relationships, and through your experiences. Capturing a vision for your future may be difficult for you now, just as it was at times in Daniel's life. Daniel is an example of having a difficult start to a young adult life; there were numerous challenges for him to conquer. He never gave up, however, but continued to strengthen his identity and his Daniel Brand. He consistently chose God and went to God to move forward. His circumstances parallel many of the mountains we must decide to climb and the decisions that face us too.

PRISCILLA AND AQUILA

> *He began to speak boldly in the synagogue. When Priscilla and Aquila heard him, they invited him to their home and explained to him the way of God more adequately* (Acts 18:26).

About two decades after the time of Jesus, in 52 A.D., the Roman emperor Claudius ordered all Jews out of the city of Rome. He was blaming the Jews, at least in part, for some recent uprisings in the city, and to clean house he took the drastic measure of ordering all Jews to leave. In that group was a man named Aquila and his wife Priscilla who, as a couple, were successful in the business of manufacturing tents. Apparently they had become followers of Jesus while in Rome, sometime before they are first mentioned in God's Word. They left

Italy and made their way to the coastal town of Corinth in south-central Greece.

At least one of them learned the tentmaking trade when they were younger, and they now worked together to sew tents and sell them to local customers. Similar to Lydia, they most certainly had a variety of customers, including those who bought new tents, and perhaps they made repairs to tents as well. The rigors of business life no doubt followed Priscilla and Aquila. Emergency repairs, upset customers, and the continual work of making new tents would have been day-to-day tasks as they worked together. Just like an individual in the working world today, they certainly had both good and bad days in their business.

Beyond their tent business, this husband and wife were extremely devoted to God. After relocating to Corinth, they met Paul, a fellow tentmaker and fellow disciple of Jesus. Their common craft (another example of how God had prepared them for this relationship long ago) brought them together as Paul worked and stayed with them as well. But it was their commitment to Christ that was the anchor for their budding relationship. With their common foundation and shared priorities, we see Paul's friendship with the married couple highlighted at multiple points in Paul's New Testament letters, giving us several insights into the combined character of these married disciples of Jesus.

After meeting Paul and spending some time with him in Corinth, Priscilla and Aquila traveled with him to the east, across the Aegean Sea, landing in Ephesus. Of course, they still had a tight bond, but Paul decided to move on from Ephesus while Priscilla and Aquila stayed in in that city strengthening the church there.

You never know when God will open a door for you with a coworker, neighbor, or longtime friend who has not found true faith in God. Thus, it's crucial to continually invest in your firm foundation, spending much time in prayer and Bible study for ever-increasing faith and conviction. Keep a mind-set of personal ministry so you are ready to share the truth with the people God puts in your path.

We see this was true for Priscilla and Aquila, as one day they listened to a man named Apollos, who was known to be knowledgeable about Jesus but probably not in an entirely correct way. Apollos may have been intimidating to some; he spoke loudly and with "great fervor" about Jesus. Many listened to him, but he was incorrect in some of his teachings.

At the beginning of this section, we read about the moment when Priscilla and Aquila reached out to Apollos in Acts 18, inviting him into their home. This invitation reminds us of the time Lydia asked Paul into her home. Apollos had an open heart to the love of Jesus shown to him by this couple, who explained the way of God in a better way. As we saw with Lydia, inviting someone into your life and showing them love and hospitality can build bridges in relationships. It is not always easy to give of yourself in this way, but it is worth it. For Priscilla and Aquila, love and hospitality became part of their brand and a real strength that inspires us today.

In three letters spanning the next several years, Paul included salutations either to this couple or from them. These references suggest their relationship with Paul was a tight one, and their engagement in Christianity did not lessen. Their relationships with other Christians were an inspiration to those in their congregations and to those in other cities at the time.

> *(55 A.D.) Aquila and Priscilla greet you warmly in the Lord, and so does the church that meets at their house* (1 Corinthians 16:19).
>
> *(57 A.D.) Greet Priscilla and Aquila, my fellow workers in Christ Jesus. They risked their lives for me. Not only I but all the churches of the Gentiles are grateful to them* (Romans 16:3, 4).
>
> *(66 A.D.) Greet Priscilla and Aquila . . .* (2 Timothy 4:19).

While they used their God-given skills of tentmaking to support themselves, their priority was the work of God. They had a dream to be used together by God, but not necessarily to make tents. The Priscilla and Aquila Brand was teamwork, togetherness, love, hospitality, and personal ministry. They are yet another example of career, working people making an impact on the world with the gifts and skills God gave them.

THEIR BRAND, YOUR BRAND

Just as these four examples clearly display godly men and women who had talents and gifts to offer the world around them, you have the same. Their backgrounds differed as God uniquely prepared them for their future roles. He is doing the same with your one-of-a-kind story. Their brands expressed who they were as they displayed God in their jobs with their coworkers, bosses, and the people around them. They used their faith, talents, and skills for His cause. They were not about just saying the right things or pretending to be godly while secretly living with an alter ego. Their brands were inspiring and filled with integrity, honesty, love, humility, and the openness that comes from living in the light.

They are incredible case studies for you as you think about launching into your career and the rest of your life. Nehemiah, the cupbearer to the king, was honest and full of integrity. He was organized, disciplined, and a hard worker. Lydia, the dealer in purple cloth, was driven, confident, and friendly. Her impact on Paul was so powerful that we read about it today. Daniel, the administrator to the king and a dream interpreter, was excellent at his work. He never gave up on God or persevering with God to get through difficult days. Priscilla and Aquila, the tentmakers, were loving and hospitable. Their giving and personal ministry were a higher call to the faithful around them, and it provides the same upward call to us today.

While you may feel a bit overwhelmed in trying to imitate these Bible heroes, their experiences probably resonate with you at the same time. All of these men and women had good days and bad days. Some had bosses and coworkers who were of a different faith or had no faith at all. Some had tragic things happen to them, close associates lie to them, or had coworkers out to undermine them and show them in a bad light. Some received promotions and rewards.

Whatever the case—all had their unique high points and no doubt weaknesses as well—they were people whose strong foundations defined their brand while they worked as career men and women. Let their brands inspire the ________________________________ Brand today and as you move forward.

PART III

Taking Action to Move Forward

Chapter Six

PRACTICAL PLANNING AND SPIRITUAL CHOICES

"So I say to you: ***Ask*** *and it will be given to you;* ***seek*** *and you will find;* ***knock*** *and the door will be opened to you. For everyone who asks receives; the one who seeks finds; and to the one who knocks, the door will be opened"* (Luke 11:9, 10, emphasis ours).

We hope you have started a journey of discovery, an inner urging toward dreaming and a call toward planning and action. We encourage you to remember your beginning and how God has deliberately prepared you for something. He has invited you to walk with Him and gives you the gift to imagine and soar toward a wonderful future full of faith and success. Just as a tree is firmly planted in the ground, to have a godly impact in your work and with your friends and family your faith must be firmly rooted in God's Word. Your prayer and Bible study must dig deeper to see and understand that God indeed is the Alpha and Omega. And your personal ministry should imitate that of Jesus so that you love to give to those around you and offer them a chance to have a relationship with God themselves.

The last two chapters were about you. For some, knowing oneself can be tricky; for others it comes more naturally. Either way, we expect that if you have completed the exercises and journaling opportunities in the *Action Planner,* or if you've just taken a step back for self-assessment, these things have helped toward that end. When you have a better picture of the person you see in the mirror, your career and other life choices will become more apparent and evident. Investing in the work of self-awareness and self-assessment will guide you in the types of jobs you seek as well as help shape your brand.

Putting deliberate effort into all of these things is the harder road, but it is very much worth the effort. It is easier to get a job, but it's harder to find the right career path. It's easier to let life come at you, harder to create your opportunity. It's easier to take your character for granted, harder to address your weaknesses to build an attractive personal brand equity. Taking the days as they come without a plan is like starting a dinner party without any recipes. You end up with food, but not the meaningful meal you intended. And even the best of intention, planning, and follow-through will not keep you from deep challenges.

In recent weeks, we (both Phil and Beth) have had a number of conversations with energized and hopeful full-time students or those already in full-time employment who are trying their best to move forward but find themselves a bit unsure of their paths. These friends are facing strong forces that seem to be working against them. We helped a friend with a bachelor's degree who, at 24, didn't like his field of study and wanted to move to a different—but unknown—career path. We talked with 24- and 25-year-old young adults (in separate conversations) who had romantic interests but were unsure how to handle them and wanted advice on how to spiritually approach their feelings. Another discussion involved a 27-year-old still working on her degree and having a tough time in one of her classes. Another was considering construction trades as a path but unsure how to make that happen. Still others had college major changes to consider or needed help in balancing academics and campus ministry. Some just needed help with their resumes.

We've also connected recently with post-university working

friends who are struggling with the challenges of career, relationships, and spirituality. One young man had been on his job for about a year and a half, but he did not like his boss and the extra hours required were severely impacting his new marriage and even church and social activities. Another wanted to reach out to her coworkers and invite them to church, but there were only five others in this small company, and she was unsure how to provide the best opportunity for them. The list of people we can all help continues.

The path is never clear-cut. What all these people have in common, however, is a mutual desire to be used by God with their whole lives while also dealing with the practical realities of making that happen in a way in which they feel fulfilled and moving forward.

To aid your course in launching your life, we thought it wise to give direction and advice on topics that have often arisen in our family or with people we know. This chapter offers practical tips about planning and the spiritual choices that support a first career, as well as other areas of life. If you feel as though you need help in one specific area or another, you are not alone. While your situation is as unique as you are, and thus some specific advice here may not be applicable, we expect you will find helpful guiding principles throughout.

You are probably now, or will soon be, at a life juncture in which there are big decisions to make. Life is about choices. At the start of each day, while your morning routine on the whole may become a habit, you begin to make choices. You choose what clothes to wear and what to eat. You choose what early conversations you have and what you say. You choose to put your faith in an awesome God—or not. You choose to study the Bible or reach out to a friend. Small choices fill the day and lead us to the more significant choices of a college major, where to live, our relationships, and beyond. Life is about choices.

ADVICE

You want to make the best decisions; we're sure of that. At times, however, we can make poor choices that set us back, delay progress, or dishearten us as we see results unfold. The enemy would love to hold you back with discouragement. Thus, our first practical tip is the essential nature of getting help from time to time. Seeking advice from those who can help is a tremendous asset in making wise decisions. There is no shortage of biblical evidence to support our need for seeking help.

> *The way of fools seems right to them, but the wise listen to advice* (Proverbs 12:15).

> *Where there is strife, there is pride, but wisdom is found in those who take advice* (Proverbs 13:10).

> *Listen to advice and accept discipline, and at the end you will be counted among the wise* (Proverbs 19:20).

> *Plans are established by seeking advice; so if you wage war, obtain guidance* (Proverbs 20:18).

Everything starts with the Alpha and Omega. We began this chapter with memorable words Jesus spoke to His disciples as an answer to their question about how to pray. We highlighted certain words because of the importance of understanding the depth of Jesus' statement. The three words—*ask, seek, knock*—are action words. If you want the door opened, you raise your arm and knock on God's door. If you want to find, you open your Bible and seek God. If you want to receive, you open your mouth and ask God. God blesses people around the world daily, according to His will, without being asked. But Jesus speaks very clearly in these words that He hears our specific prayers as we pour out our hearts to God. We don't just pray to be blessed, however. We pray to connect with the creator of the universe, the one who gave us life and breath. We connect so that we can better understand ourselves, our purpose, and the God we serve. It's likely you are reading this book to search God, know His heart, and grasp His meaning for your life. That begins with talking to God and asking, seeking, and knocking.

In your prayers, go after it! Start with a decision to have a humble heart and be open to God's answer. Ask God for clear direction in your life so you can make great choices. Pray that God will move in such a way that you can see the barriers that may hinder your progress and have the wisdom and strength to overcome. And decide to never, ever quit.

In chapter three we discussed the Parable of the Persistent Widow found in Luke 18. The lesson is to never stop asking and seeking in our prayers. You may know the feeling or temptation to abandon prayer. Almost without noticing, we can slide into quitting if we don't see or feel God's answer, or if we are only halfhearted in our desires. We'd like to see God's response on a billboard while driving down the highway, receive an email reply directly from the Almighty, or receive a text directly from Him that gives us ultra-clear direction. It doesn't work that way, however. And when answers we are seeking don't happen according to our will or timing, we can get frustrated and lose faith in our prayers and either spend less time in prayer or, sadly, quit altogether.

Asking to follow God's path for your steps is one request you can pray daily, however, and with no end! To put it in more visual terms, if you stood a good distance away from a friend while having a conversation with them, it would be hard, maybe even impossible, to hear and comprehend. But if you are close to them, standing face to face, you see and understand. Similarly, the closer we are to God in our prayers the better we will be able to see and hear Him. If you have been through difficult circumstances in the past that make prayer a struggle for you, journal about those times and talk with others you know who pray faithfully. Our trust issues can make us wary of vulnerability and transparency with others and with God as well. If prayer is hard, get help and ask others to assist you. Whether you've been a Christian for five days or five years, if you have roadblocks to prayer, they can derail your ultimate journey of knowing God and finding His will for your life. Your ultimate desire is to connect with the Almighty in heart, mind, and soul, and, ultimately, to create a career that brings Him glory. That journey begins, and is sustained by, prayer.

To complement the idea of asking, seeking, and knocking in your prayer life, God has put people in your life to help. We recommend a thoughtful approach to getting advice from qualified people around you. Think specifically about your decision space and who can help. Depending on your needs, some people are better suited for information than others. For instance, would you want to get advice on a college major change from someone who has never attended college? Would you seek financial help from someone who is irresponsible with money? Two easy examples, right? The answers to both questions: of course not. Therefore, consider your source. Talk to people who are already in a successful career path you are considering. If you are changing majors or careers, find others who have made that move successfully. If you are having trouble overcoming an obstacle in creating your future, find a person who has overcome a similar barrier. If you need help in finances, find someone who manages money with excellence. We mention this because it can be easy to settle for the convenient friend for empathy, sympathy, and advice rather than the person who can help you move forward. Inevitably, talking to more than one person will yield different opinions and information. Receiving multiple views is an excellent strategy to help you consider the big picture (Proverbs 11:14, 15:22, 24:6). Consider your sources and their advice and do your best to make the best choices. You are the one who will live with the decision, and the great news is that God is always at work within those choices, teaching us and strengthening us. Lastly under this section, books are also helpful to inform and educate.

PERSISTENCE: NEVER GIVE UP

> *When Peter saw him, he asked, "Lord, what about him?" Jesus answered, "If I want him to remain alive until I return, what is that to you? You must follow me"* (John 21:21, 22).

In this moment, John was trailing some distance behind as Peter walked with Jesus. Jesus had just talked with Peter about the massive effort that would be needed to stay faithful during the difficult challenges that lay ahead. The words shook Peter. In a possible attempt to defuse the feelings, or maybe to see if it was going to be as hard for others as it would be for himself, Peter, glancing at John, turned to Jesus and asked, "What about that guy?" In a heartbeat, Jesus stopped both men in their tracks and turned to look deep into Peter's eyes. Jesus knew this would be a life-defining moment that Peter would never forget. With intense conviction, possibly a deeper tone, and perhaps even a pointed finger on Peter's chest, Jesus delivers the words we read above. For a moment, put yourself in Peter's sandals, with Jesus looking solely into your eyes. Fully embrace and take to heart His words: "You must follow me." It is a call for commitment, a call to stay focused.

These words have long been a meaningful passage for us (Phil and Beth) because of the enemy's constant efforts to make us quit on God. We've had our battles. Since our Christianity began, we have had experiences that nearly crushed our spirits. We've had close friends leave to live in other cities or countries, and others who have left their faith. We've had career, financial, and relational struggles. We've had health struggles and surgeries. While some weeks and months seemed like uphill climbs, we've also enjoyed the mountain peaks at the end. Our experiences have varied far more than we would have imagined, and the life journey we saw ahead decades ago has taken far different paths to place us where we are today. Along the way, in a strange dichotomy, some of our biggest joys *and* hurts have come from those relationships closest to us. We have trusted in the good days, which most of them have been, that God continues to mold us in His hands as a potter molds a jar of clay. In our shortcomings, the harder days have brought misgivings toward God's attentiveness, but still we persevere. It has all been much different than we ever expected! Perhaps that's the same point Jesus was trying to help Peter understand.

Our journey is not unique to what others face. Our friends share the same sentiments. While feeling mostly blessed and joyful, life hasn't always gone as they thought it would. It's helpful to remember the Lord's words and implant them in our souls: "You must follow me." About thirty years ago, we listened to a speaker share a lesson about the importance of enduring in one's relationship with God. With deep conviction, he shared a line we still remember: "I don't know what will happen tomorrow, but I know that I won't leave God!" That was the very attitude Jesus was trying to cultivate in Peter. As mentioned, we've closely held to this thought, and it has sustained us in the rising floods that life has brought.

We do not know where tomorrow will take you, but there are some things we can promise. Just as it has been for us, our peers, and all who have gone before us, our lives will have challenges. Some will be more daunting and difficult than we would like. You will have cause for both celebration and despair. You may suddenly lose a job or experience financial hardship. Someone close to you may lose their life. The dark days may include friends who will decide to make other choices in their faith or inadvertently hurt you.

But remember the words of the Lord: "You must follow me." Give your full heart to God. Don't let anyone or anything take that from you. You are too valuable and the stakes of your life on earth and your eternal soul are just too high. Continue to build your foundation so you can always stand on it. Decide today, tomorrow, the next day, and every day after that you will not be swayed by the lies and deceptions of the enemy. Don't let your circumstances or the choices of others cause you to waver in faith and steadfastness. Instead, wholeheartedly follow Jesus until the end.

PRIORITIES

> *"In the same way, any of you who does not give up everything he has cannot be my disciple"* (Luke 14:33).

We have discussed being "all in" with God, working as if for the Lord with all our hearts, and wholeheartedly following as God desires.

This passage follows the same theme and is a clear indication of Jesus' desire for people's hearts, not simply for greater numbers of people. Verse 25 of this same chapter describes a large crowd that was following Jesus during the time He made this hard statement, and many in the crowd chose to leave. Jesus' words were consistent: He said it would require an individual's full heart to be His disciple. This occasion was no different, and statements like this one probably angered or dismayed many, even to the point of leaving. Many liked Jesus' teachings, some came for the food, and most were amazed by the miracles—but very few gave Him their whole heart.

But if someone has given up everything to be a disciple of Jesus, how does it work when they are a university student or company employee? Are they a disciple of Jesus first or a student first? Is their work the top priority or is God the number one priority? If they have lab work for chemistry or need to travel out of town for a meeting, is it acceptable to skip a church event?

We've seen these very questions turned into a playground for the enemy. The struggle is legitimate. A faithful follower of Jesus knows that the Lord should have their full heart and learns more and more how that shows up in day-to-day living. But legitimate responsibilities can tug at that commitment, pulling one's heart in multiple directions. And if the enemy can cause confusion or misdirection, maybe add in some bad advice, then perhaps he can distract the eyes from a focus on Jesus. No easy answers or advice works the same for all circumstances. The Bible clearly demands "Jesus is Lord," but we live in this world and need to provide for ourselves. Wisdom from the Bible and others is required.

Think back to the Proverbs 31 Woman and to several of the biblical characters we have studied so far. In the case of Daniel, Nehemiah, Priscilla and Aquila, and the Proverbs 31 Woman, these people were clearly used by God through their work. The Proverbs 31 Woman was explicitly noted for her character, hard work, and love of God. God used Daniel's education to His glory. These were not "either-or" lives. If you had asked them if they were employees or students first, or if

God was first, they might have looked at you with a tilt of the head like a dog that doesn't understand! Remember your full life is meant to be in service of God. If you are a disciple of Jesus, why would your education be opposed to God? Or a church activity? Instead, would you not be called to a higher standard in your studies? The same goes for being employed. Should you not be a better employee so your workmates can see your commitment and Jesus' lordship in your life in the workplace?

Specific to the university lifestyle, we have seen students in the dilemma of choosing to study versus taking time to reach out to fellow students or attend a church midweek meeting. For university students, these problems often stem from a lack of discipline during the day when they have time. Staying up until 2 a.m. for a pointless chat with friends leading to a noon sleep-in the next morning is not helpful. Not doing a thorough job with your homework throughout the semester when there is time to work on it, causing an extremely late night before the test in hopes of squeaking out a C, is thoughtless and does not glorify God. Our suggestion is to approach your college studies like a full-time job. Accomplishing schoolwork during the daytime often leaves free time for self and ministry in the evenings.

As Christians who desire a strong foundation, we should want to be at services and small group meetings (Hebrews 10:25) and do all we can to make it happen. Having a disciplined spirit about academics will help minimize the moments when academics come in conflict with spiritual commitments.

If you're employed, you may have out-of-town travel or late meetings that extend your time commitment to your work. We (Phil and Beth) have certainly had those types of commitments. We encourage you to remember that work life is not separate from the spiritual life. Our whole life is in service to God. Extra commitments to work may be required, and we should fulfill them dutifully, as if working for the Lord. As you get advice from spiritual advisors, it can be helpful for them to reflect on whether you may be slipping into a job dynamic that makes it hard to fulfill a Christian lifestyle in the body of Christ simply because it doesn't allow you to do so. In this circumstance, it is often appropriate to consider a job or career change.

Careers, education, social events, and more all take time commitments, but these shouldn't be the fields where we keep our treasure. Ultimately, one's heart needs to be entirely devoted to God as a Christian. If there are conflicting time schedules that are temporary such as a single class that interferes with a worship service for a few months, it is probably not a significant issue. If you are in a more permanent circumstance that conflicts often, perhaps you should consider a change. Again, reach out to those who know you best and have your truest interest in mind.

RELATIONSHIPS

These are, arguably, the backbone of success in life. Relationships fill your life, and they mean something to you every day. Having a growing relationship with God, your family, a trusted friend, your wife or husband, your children, or with a coworker—these are just the beginning. These people and so many more can be the very support network you need to launch your life now and carry your life momentum into the future. Ironically, however, close relationships can also be the cause of the biggest hurts and setbacks. Therefore, we thought it wise to discuss your most critical relationships. This section is not a comprehensive list, nor do we intend this as professional psychological help. Instead, we intend here simple discussions that may help your perspective as you transition into long-term life outside of high school and college.

GOD

It all starts with your relationship with God. We have already discussed the foundation formula and shown examples in God's Word of how working adult people in the Bible loved Him and leaned on Him throughout their lives. Be wise, however, and understand that this loving relationship started with God Himself, and not with the good deeds of those people.

> *For God so loved the world that he gave his one and only Son, that whoever believes in him shall not perish but have eternal life. For God did not send his Son into the world to condemn the world, but to save the world through him* (John 3:16, 17).

> *We love because he first loved us* (1 John 4:19).

The clearer your perspective is on how God reached out to you just because He loved you and desired a relationship with you, the clearer you will be in other areas of your life. This understanding takes deliberate thought and meditation to understand that you don't deserve that relationship. You have not excelled enough or done such spectacular things that God offers you a relationship with Him. Your character is not superior, nor is it deserving. In our humanity, we have earned quite the opposite (Romans 6:23) of receiving a gift from God. It is God who loved us, God who has given to us, and God who desired us first.

We cannot underscore enough how having an ever-increasing appreciation for this relationship will guide and help you through all others. While you will enjoy so many benefits from great friends, coworkers, and family, the reality is that, at times, people will let you down, even those closest to you. Some will undercut you and hurt you deliberately, but at other times the hurt will actually work to your good. The pain will come at various times and in differing ways, so expect it, with a forgiving heart, as God has forgiven you. Keep your eyes fixed on Jesus and continue to build the foundation. God is the rock, the mainstay. Do not let the enemy convince you otherwise as you continue your life pursuits.

PARENTS OR GUARDIANS

All of us have a wide variety of memories from our childhood. Some had a lovingly supportive upbringing, others less so, and some faced significant trauma in their childhood. Whether you come from a single parent home, have stepparents, foster parents, guardians, or traditional mothers and fathers, there is one aspect of parenting and guardianship that has become an obstacle for many. We want to address it here.

As you grow and mature, those who helped you when you were younger may be having a difficult time letting go, or you may be having a hard time growing into an adult relationship with that authority figure. It is probably not a coincidence that the rise of "helicopter parents," or guardians of that same nature, hanging on longer than they should coincides with the growth of the information age. Parents and their children have instant access, all the time, to what each other are doing and experiencing as they grow. This access can cause difficulty when the child is growing into an adult and needs to make her or his own decisions, reap the consequences of those choices, and develop character and a life path. Parents may over-involve themselves in activities, responsibilities, and choices that adult children should be making more independently. This continued engagement can lead to the adult child second-guessing their decisions, being paralyzed by fear, and generally "waiting for life to show up" instead of moving forward with established intentions.

Whatever the fundamental cause, our experience has shown that this issue has produced young adults often lacking the needed basic skills in problem-solving and often without the spirit of grit needed to fight through challenges. When distress comes, a helicopter parent or guardian will swoop in and make the calls or fill out the paperwork to sort it all out, leaving the adult child without the skills, courage, and desire to figure out how to resolve issues themselves. As a young adult, you can probably see where this could become an issue with your future, or perhaps you have already found yourself in these circumstances.

As you launch your life, you'll have troubles on your journey, and the difficulties will probably become more common than you would like. At times, the challenges may seem impossible; there may not seem a way out. For example, at the same time you're planning your next few years, you may be having trouble in your academics, misgivings about your new boss, or discouraged about something a close friend said to you. Your dream to soar may require that you overcome your debt, transition to a new university, or deal with a malfunctioning car. Or your college major may not have provided the great job you thought it would when you first started, and now you feel stuck. All of these are common problems.

The first step does not always need to be a call to your parents or someone else to solve your problem for you. Consider the alternative. Start with prayers to God to strengthen yourself, then look in your mirror. That person is probably more capable of dealing with this challenge than you may think. When you find yourself stuck in a life circumstance, your first thoughts should be about you masterminding a solution or two. You develop a plan to solve your debt problem, switch majors or classes, fix your car trouble, or figure out how to work in a job that isn't the right fit. Then get advice from those who can help. Talk to your academic advisor, your mentor at work, your guardians. If your parent(s) want to swoop in to rescue, maybe you should respectfully tell them, "No, I got it!" Transferring your troubles to others without you figuring out a plan is juvenile and a disservice to yourself and your growth process. You may not exactly know what the solution is for your current problem, but challenge yourself to come up with options. Show maturity, be solution-oriented, and then seek advice. The transition to professional life, adulthood, or any post-high school plan can and will be difficult. If you don't plan to grab hold of it, it will grab hold of you and tie you up in troubles. Put some intention together and take it on. You can do it.

MENTORS

"Mentors are important, and I don't think anybody makes it in the world without some form of mentorship."
— Oprah Winfrey[9]

Oprah Winfrey is one of the most financially successful women in American history. The master of the talk show and super talented, her television program aired for twenty-five years beginning in 1986. By some accounts, she is the most influential woman in the world. Her impact in the media and television industries grew to incredible proportions while her Chicago-based show aired. Her audiences adore her for her humility and philanthropy. But Oprah would never say she did it alone. She largely credits her rise in success to her relationship with an older advisor, the late Maya Angelou. Oprah pursued the poet and author for support through many valleys and sought guidance for the challenges that were part of her life journey. Life principals, business decisions, and racial challenges are topics we are confident would have been discussed as their friendship grew. Wisdom came from the older Ms. Angelou. She turned her narrative into an example. She was a role model, sounding board, and mentor to one of the most popular and successful businesswomen in history.

Having a mentor or older advisor is very much a biblical concept. Timothy confided in Paul as a mentor, and the twelve disciples looked to Jesus, of course. (There are many more examples.) Your trusted relationships should include one or more people you look to for advice, and not just friends. If you are still taking classes at your university, the school will often provide academic and employment advisors for you. Some companies also help facilitate a mentor, and you do well to take advantage of such opportunities. Your church may facilitate a relationship or two for you. It helps, however, if you take it upon yourself to first see your need for mentoring and then pursue relationships in that capacity.

First, understand your need and the advantages of a mentor relationship. With Oprah so successful and living as an inspiration to millions, why would she want or need mentors? The truth is that wisdom from experience is irreplaceable in career, life, and character development. And what an advantage! It is not like you are the first one to live, have troubles, or face the need to make big decisions. Everyone lives through difficult experiences, and many are willing to pass on what they have learned.

If you find yourself in a job without a mentor, ask your boss who he or she might recommend. Even if you are not in your career job, seek to establish relationships with people who are in your desired field. These are networking opportunities that can build bridges to future employment, excellent references, and more. Building relationships like this will enhance your employability as you learn about your field and the needed ingredients for success. Additionally, having others in your church advise you as you grow spiritually is a must. Look to those in your ministry who you admire, as well as those ahead of you in life who you respect. Remember to ask, seek, and knock! Chase after those relationships and set up regular times with those valuable people in your life. Then allow God to work through those you trust.

We've (Phil and Beth) been fortunate to have several different mentors in our lives. Some have been Christians in our church, and some have been fellow employees we looked to for career development. Most were extremely helpful in their guidance for our careers, parenting, or other life challenges. On more than one occasion, when we pursued career advice, we received life and character advice as well! The benefits have been countless. As we look back and think about those who have helped us this far, we can see how God was molding our character and teaching us through them and with their advice. And, in turn, some of the valuable lessons we learned from our mentors are found in this book.

DATING RELATIONSHIPS

Dating relationships can be a lot of fun; entering such a relationship can be an exhilarating time of life. We offer a few thoughts because such a relationship can have a direct impact on your career, and it can impact how you feel about yourself and your relationship with God. As you launch your life, we hope your dating will enhance the process. Having a boyfriend or girlfriend exposes your character, can breathe life into your faithfulness, and gives you a spring in your step.

But the enemy, prowling like a lion to pounce on you, can twist and turn your thoughts, all in an effort to snatch your soul. There are many influences you will feel.

> *Therefore, with minds that are alert and fully sober, set your hope on the grace to be brought to you when Jesus Christ is revealed at his coming. As obedient children, do not conform to the evil desires you had when you lived in ignorance. But just as he who called you is holy, so be holy in all you do; for it is written: "Be holy, because I am holy"* (1 Peter 1:13-16).

Like so much of essential Christianity, Christian dating should look much different than that of the world. Peter's insight into the mindset mentioned above should impact us since the world has taught us all poor habits. Peter calls us out of the world by telling us to avoid evil desires and to be obedient and holy. This change takes deliberate action on your part. You can't live honorably without entirely turning away from unrighteousness living. It never works like the movies or the Hallmark Channel—these things can provide some fun viewing, but they usually display everything working out all right and everyone being happy and together in the end. It certainly is not like *The Bachelor*, where women or men contestants throw themselves at a prospective mate, and, in a climactic finish, choose the one who flirted and kissed the best, calling that love. The influence on our culture that these and many more shows like them have is horrible. They are a considerable discredit to what can be a real blessing from God.

Your friendship circle will also influence your view. It doesn't matter if it is a large circle or a small one. A healthy and supportive friendship is a great blessing. Those closest to you know you best and can be helpful advisors. Dating is personal and needs a degree of maturity. Look to people you admire and create an inner circle of trusted advisors. Watch couples who have healthy marriages and dating relationships and seek out time with them.

In the twentysomething culture today, it seems the casual "taking a girl or guy out on a date or double date" is a bit under attack. Perhaps it is a combination of TV shows and movies, as we mentioned earlier, or the enormous ease, availability, and debilitating use of pornography that are among the worst contributors to this mind-set. Or perhaps the decrease in actual face-to-face social interaction of growing adolescents and young adults is a culprit as well. So often men and women feel they are in the "friend zone" and take it personally when they do not instantly match with an interest. Sometimes we think we should live in an online environment like the Tinder world, where someone falls in love with us at first sight. Apps like Snapchat and others allow men and women to utilize impure pictures to acquire or keep an interest. These worldly influences and dynamics produce lies of expectations and extreme discouragement when desires are not met. They also encourage impurity and immorality to build intimacy. Simply put, these enemy tactics do not work and are against God's laws and will.

We recommend plenty of casual and double dating to build a genuine friendship that God can grow into a romantic one. To engage in this, you may need to set your phone down and talk to the person of interest face to face! Our culture is moving too quickly and easily to modes of communication that are only done from a distance. Use the audio mode on your phones or, better yet, talk to the other person directly and ask how their day is going, or ask about their favorite class or restaurant. Ask where they have traveled or where they've lived. Want to know more? Ask why geometry is their favorite class, or why the local pizzeria is their favorite place to hang out. If you're nervous about talking with them, you are a member of a very large club! There is nothing inherently wrong with a text. But far too many hide behind a digital message and do not face their anxieties with face-to-face conversations.

Let's get a little more into specifics. Let's learn from Peter and not live according to the world! First, view casual dating as a no-pressure friendship and fun time. Go out to activities where you can have conversations. Perhaps dinner and a walk through a park. We strongly suggest going with a friend and making it a double date. Talk about your past week or what dreams you have on your heart. You can discuss what you like or dislike about your classes or work, but have a fun, lighthearted time. You can explain the things you've read in this book and how you're going to launch your life. It can be a lot of fun just talking about what the future may hold for each of you. Playing card games, throwing a Frisbee, or walking a dog are all great ideas for a double date, and two to three hours will be plenty. And as a side note, to the guys: you would do well to open the doors for her. Treat her like a queen; she is God's daughter. At the end of the date, we recommend a side-by-side hug along with words of encouragement, and no more. You may be tempted to do more, but trust us: this is best.

As you consider planning your future and launching your life, a steady boyfriend or girlfriend may enter the scene. After you've had an initial date with someone, you may have noticed that your relationship clicked quite well. You came home from the date and thought that you would like to do that again! Look at it like you are in the process of gaining another friend. As your relationship grows, the amount of contact during the week via text, phone calls, or other means becomes a common question. Each person's thoughts and relationships differ, but in the beginning, we suggest that less is more. That means a lesser amount of "during the week" contact in the beginning weeks of the relationship will lead to better face-to-face conversations on dates. This moderation also helps keep the relationship at an appropriate distance so you can explore the relationship with complete purity.

Let's turn to the step of choosing to date steady. Select someone who has similar dreams or has goals that are a good match. In general, we encourage you to focus on launching your life, and when that comes together with another person who is launching theirs in a similar direction, you have a good match.

We offer three pieces of advice during a steady dating relationship. First: walk very closely with God. Build your foundation formula so you can be clear-minded in your big decisions. Second: seek plenty of advice from godly people you admire. As discussed earlier, God blesses a humble heart who seeks wisdom from other men and women of God. Third: be pure. The world throws so much at you. Don't give in. Don't go to places you shouldn't on your computer or phone. And more importantly, do not touch your partner in places you shouldn't reach. Don't put yourself in compromising situations where hormones take over, where you lose your commitments to purity. Be diligent in this and don't soften your biblical convictions. Allowing sin in your relationship is a sure recipe for God to not bless it, leading to wrong choices and actions that will haunt you and possibly devastate your partner.

We (Phil and Beth) went on several double dates while attending college, about once, twice, or three times a month, and with a host of people. Most were just for fun and encouragement with no further intentions. We each had a steady dating relationship with others before our first date, but those both ended after a short time. We knew each other and had talked a little for a couple of years, but there was one notable October Sunday when we bumped into each other in the aisle after a worship service. Our first date was exactly one week later, after the next Sunday worship. We went to lunch with our double dates and took a stroll through a park where the autumn leaves were colorful, playful. Neither of us would ever go on another date with anyone else.

After one and a half years of steady dating, we married after nine weeks of engagement. That's the start of a great story, but it's also for another book. We want you to have a similar story that entails a pure dating relationship, a courtship focused on God, and a future brimming with hopes and dreams. It is up to you to set the standard and have deep convictions about your future relationships.

JOB SEARCHING, RESUMES, INTERVIEWING

"The best way to predict the future is to create it."
— Abraham Lincoln[10]

Nancy Lincoln hoped for a better future and more opportunities for her children than she had for herself or her husband, Thomas. To that end, although not formally educated, she spent substantial time reading to Abraham and Sarah, her two young children. While still maintaining the home, Nancy made reading a daily priority. Sometimes it was the Bible, but there were other books too, and she was committed to helping her children grow. Sadly, when Abraham was just 9 and Sarah only 7, Nancy passed away suddenly after contracting a disease known at the time as "milk sickness." As you might imagine, this life-defining moment for the future United States president and his sister would never be forgotten. But the tragic ending to this mother's life was not the end of her legacy. The small spark Nancy created was enough to light a fire for her son.

It would be up to the young Abraham, however, to continue his education. His father, Thomas, was not of the same mind when it came to education, and he promptly put Abraham to work on the farm, ignoring the child's desire to read and learn more. Against the will of his father, who saw no use in reading books, the future president still found a way to read and discover. He spent much of his teen years being creative in overcoming the resistance he faced, especially as his mind-set grew in a separate direction from that of his father. As his relationship with his father weakened, Abraham would walk miles to a neighboring town just to get his next book.[11] His drive and efforts led to new opportunities as he started his public service career while just in his early twenties. And, of course, eventually he became the sixteenth president and the central figure in one of the most defining times in the history of the United States of America.

The quote above is powerful when you learn more about Abraham Lincoln. He made the statement because he *lived* it; he did not let the many difficulties he faced sway him from his course.

In the same way, when it comes to your finalizing your resume and launching your job search, things will probably prove more difficult than you want them to be. But you can create opportunities for yourself if you put in the effort.

As before, we believe you can achieve the big picture of landing a job that is in service of God's plan for your life on the premise of *ask*, *seek*, and *knock*. These thoughts in Luke suggest proactive, intentional work on our part to allow God to open a door, and they are applicable to set your course in your life and career.

Let's talk resume first. We believe there are two primary requirements for writing a great resume. First, you must know who you are (in the big context of your life) and how God has prepared you. Second, you need to do the work it takes to represent that *you*, brilliantly, in a one-page document. You must represent yourself so well that your resume is noteworthy and attractive. Often it will need to stand out relative to hundreds of other resumes.

Sometimes we want the magic light bulb to come on and illuminate the perfect job, or we think it's a simple ask and then our desire just shows up from God. In the end, you have to do the work. Think about James 2:17: "In the same way, faith by itself, if it is not accompanied by action, is dead." And James 2:22, 24: "You see that his [Abraham's] faith and his actions were working together, and his faith was made complete by what he did. . . . You see that a person is considered righteous by what they do and not by faith alone." Asking requires us to know ourselves and know what to ask of God. You need to be grounded in the details of your ideal job so you can pray specifically. Seeking requires extraordinary effort to go after something and persevere when achieving it isn't easy. You may face rejection in job searching in not getting an interview, or you may advance as far as being the second choice when there is only one job available. Regardless, remember this: knocking implies putting yourself out there and taking a risk. You need to cast a wide net of applications to land a job that contributes to a growing resume.

There are many resources available for resume writing. This book wasn't written with the goal of being an authority on the subject. Instead, our book attempts to help you capture the whole version of yourself, including those Christian and discipleship character qualities that are the traits needed to make you both attractive and desirable as a hire. Our goal is not to help you evangelize or proselytize through your resume. Instead, our goal is to help you create a resume that represents your gifts and spiritual qualities so the reader gets a sense of your character. Your character has positive attributes that are spiritual and include an upward call to righteousness. And those attributes are desirable to potential hiring managers.

Many times, when we (Phil and Beth) look at the first drafts of resumes, we see a list of generic tasks that describe a basic job. Many times those listed jobs may not be the kinds of experience that jump off the page for hiring managers. We also find when consulting with various writers of resumes that successful resumes usually speak to two things: first, why a candidate is valuable because of his or her character; second, why that job suited the candidate's strengths.

Having a resume that speaks to godly qualities like patience, perseverance, generosity, great work ethic or attitude, service, appreciating people, and so on—well, these are great things to highlight. It makes your resume more of the story about the ____________________ Brand rather than just a list of tasks you did in generic jobs or service experiences. As you add character to your resume, you will cut through the clutter of the resume stack to be the one who gets called for an interview because more of *you* is on the page. Be assured that your godly character matters in a job over the long haul. It makes you more interesting in a resume and will separate you from that stack on the hiring manager's desk. You have gifts, talents, and character. Your job is to make them come alive in your resume.

Creative use of words also enhances a resume. As you fill in details of your experiences, start the bullet points with action words. Don't use boring words like "did," "was," or "completed." Instead, use higher impact verbs and descriptive words like "achieved," "improved," or "managed." If you can monetize your contribution in some way with a number, incorporate that in the bullet point. For example: "Improved the customer base by 20 percent by exceptional customer service and relational skills"; or, "Initiated and created a sales system so that the volume of widgets sold increased by 40 percent." Each experience you list on your resume should tell a small story about the ______________________ Brand and cause the resume reader to want to have a conversation with you about it.

As you draft your resume, reach out to your mentors. It can be quite helpful if they have previously hired and fired employees or if they are in your field or at least close to your field. Beyond resume input, ask these people if they know of open jobs or places to search for jobs in your desired field. As you do that, these relationships can grow into networking and mentoring relationships that can fuel your career going forward. And remember to reach out to people who will tell you the truth and offer constructive feedback. Take the extra step that others don't when looking for a job. Let mentors review your resume and help you practice interviewing. Embracing the people who will give you honest and open feedback will set you apart and give you an advantage.

As you finalize your resume, start planning and practice interviewing. Good interviewing involves preparation on two fronts. First, be prepared to answer questions and tell the story about why you are the right person for the job. The hiring managers want to know what you can do to make their company better. Second, be knowledgeable about both the job and the company where you are applying. Demonstrate this knowledge in the interview by offering questions. Good hires are a win-win for both parties. Good interviews have a balance of dialogue about you as well as about the job. This balanced dialogue leads to both parties being able to see if you are a strong match for the position. If you show up at an interview only prepared to discuss yourself, the interviewer will feel the discussion is one-sided, that you think the job is all about you. Even worse, you could portray yourself as if you think they are doing themselves a favor by hiring you. That pride will be evident and get you nowhere. When you demonstrate knowledge and curiosity about the job, company, or organization, the interviewers will know you have done your homework and that you have given thought to how you are going to make a difference if they hire you.

As mentioned, you should prepare well for interviews, including finding a coach, mentor, or supporter who can practice a mock interview with you. Practicing your answers multiple times out loud with another person can help your confidence, succinctness, and coherency. We can't stress enough: think about how you will help make your potential company better. Consider your success stories. Victories like how you overcame a hard class, or how you took on more work at your previous job because a coworker left, or how you had a positive impact in various group projects. In the interview, be prepared to ask one of your questions after you have answered one of theirs. Practice this two-way dialogue ahead of time.

The *Action Planner* has more help for resume writing and interviewing. There is a more extensive and detailed section with helpful resume tips, words to include and not include, and interviewing advice. The greatest thing you can do for yourself is buckle down and do the extra work. You may need to send out dozens of resumes. Be aggressive and think like Abraham Lincoln in creating your future so God can open various doors of possibilities for you.

FINANCES

"Money often costs too much."
— Ralph Waldo Emerson[12]

In this somewhat well-known saying, Emerson was not speaking of the value of money but instead the control money can have on any person, whether they have much or little. We need it to live from day to day, but money can be a distraction if we worry or focus on not having enough, or about what to do with our surplus. There are not many external things that can be as controlling as money or the love of money. We have known faithful people who worked many hours and earned a good deal of money. Their nice car fits in the garage of the lovely home they have purchased for themselves. But as time marches on their desire for more precludes their passion for God, leading to a darkness that ends in divorce, faithless children, a broken home, or a loss of faith in God. We have also seen friends struggle from paycheck to paycheck, fighting to get ahead, and this also can lead to struggles and faithlessness. It is not the dollar amount that controls us, it is the removing of our eyes from Jesus to the focus on those dollars. God knows our weaknesses and offers plenty of biblical coaching to help us set our minds on the right path.

> *For the love of money is a root of all kinds of evil. Some people, eager for money, have wandered from the faith and pierced themselves with many griefs* (1 Timothy 6:10).

> *Dishonest money dwindles away, but whoever gathers money little by little makes it grow* (Proverbs 13:11).

> *Peter answered: "May your money perish with you, because you thought you could buy the gift of God with money!"* (Acts 8:20)

> *Whoever loves money never has enough; whoever loves wealth is never satisfied with their income. This too is meaningless* (Ecclesiastes 5:10).

Whenever you begin a discussion on finances, having a proper perspective is sensible. If you are lucky enough to be hired into a strong-paying job, you know it feels good to start a new career and begin earning a sizeable paycheck from week to week. But the more money you earn the more your mind can get a bit twisted in it. It is the first time you are genuinely earning an income with which to build your life. If you are still in school or have yet to find the higher-paying job you're seeking, and are still struggling, don't be discouraged.

The world says there is happiness found in accumulating money. How many advertisements, movies, and other media have you seen or heard that portray a wealthy, happy person? If you go by what you see in the world of entertainment, it would seem that money does equal happiness. Contrary to that message, however, Jesus offers us clear words on where our hearts should be regardless of our income or how much is in our bank account.

> *"Do not store up for yourselves treasures on earth, where moth and rust destroy, and where thieves break in and steal. But store up for yourselves treasures in heaven, where moth and rust do not destroy, and where thieves do not break in and steal. For where your treasure is, there your heart will be also. The eye is the lamp*

> *of the body. If your eyes are good, your whole body will be full of light. But if your eyes are bad, your whole body will be full of darkness. How great is that darkness! No one can serve two masters. Either he will hate the one and love the other, or he will be devoted to the one and despise the other. You cannot serve both God and money"* (Matthew 6:19-24).

We have discussed how your whole life is in service of God, not just the religious part. Your view of your finances and how you handle them is part of that equation as well. Your view of money is about your character and how solid you are on your foundation. There is nothing wrong with money, having it, or even having plenty of it. But the choices you make as you launch your life and continue to grow older will expose where you genuinely store your treasure. Your character will drive your decisions on things like giving back, making purchases, and saving for the future. Will you be both wise and generous with what God has given you?

If you're still in school, or just starting out, we implore you to complete your degree as timely as possible, and with the least amount of debt. When considering taking on debt by student loans or other means, you are wise to consider the amount of debt accumulated against the job you hope to get on the back end. Let this also be a helpful guide in where you choose to attend university. Obtaining student loans to attend a high-cost private university in a major that will lead to a lower-wage career is not a good mix.

Consider the story of a young lady who set herself back financially for years, maybe decades, by choices she made years ago. She loved creativity and wanted to study marketing. She chose to attend a private school about one hour from where she grew up. At the time, the university cost about $40,000 per year, but she had no money to attend. She qualified for enough student loans to cover the entire cost. She completed her bachelor's degree in the prescribed four years but was unable to get a job. Part of her challenge in getting a job following her undergrad studies was that she chose a smaller, expensive private school that was not known for its marketing program, nor was there a strong alumni group. Additionally, the school was not that helpful in guiding her to a career. With no job offer in hand, she continued her education to obtain a master's degree in the same major at the same school. After completing the advanced degree, she was able to get a job at the university making thirteen dollars an hour. But now reality was quickly setting in. She used student loans semester after semester to pay for her education, and at the end of her university experience she had accumulated an overwhelming loan debt of well over $150,000. And the debt doesn't go away! It may take her twenty years or more to pay off these loans. The better choice would have been another university where she had initially applied and was accepted. It was about twenty minutes from her home, and that university also offered marketing in its business school. The marketing major was also rated top five in the nation at this school, sending graduates to successful careers with employers all over the world. On top of that, it was a public school, and the tuition costs were less than half that of the school she chose to attend. It is essential to consider these types of things before and during your time in college.

In your day-to-day finances, keep a simple budget. It does not need to be much, just a simple tool that will track what you spend. Get a folder and begin saving all your receipts for the month. Keep every receipt, from fast food to phone bill, from loans and cable bill to gifts and traveling. Make sure you have any credit card statements and bank account statements handy as well. Everything that has to do with finances should be in that folder from the first day of the month to the last.

Next, we suggest a simple spreadsheet with the weeks listed on the vertical column on the left side and your spending categories across the top. With each category, list your target budget amount for expenses for the week. Leave the box beside it blank, then fill it in with what you spent. The spending categories should include gas, food, utilities, rent, clothing, phone bill, insurance, car payment, contribution for your church, and may also include saving for specific future plans or the future in general. For example, if you want to keep forty dollars per month for a trip you are planning next year, be sure to put that in your budget. Important: your spending should always be less than the money you have or are planning to spend. A guide in our *Action Planner* will help you further with this. Review your receipts for accuracy and get in the habit of watching your finances on a weekly basis. When first tracking your expenditures, remember not to beat yourself up if you are initially overspending in a specific category. The point of this exercise is to recognize patterns, see where you have strengths and weaknesses, and come back to the budget each month to reassess, grow, and change. It's crucial that you check in on your spending regularly and know how you are doing so you can make better decisions and plans for your future.

Budgeting your money is essential to being responsible with your money. As mentioned, keeping track of every dollar you spend will be illuminating and help you save as you see more clearly where your money goes. Set your budget for the next four months and see how you do, or even try one year. You can always adjust your spending as needed; just don't let your budget go ignored. A little discipline in this area of your life will go a long way toward financial wisdom and making good choices with the money you have. If you're having trouble starting this process, ask someone who is good with money and budgeting to help you. Maybe consider doing it together with a roommate or friend; it can be an enlightening and empowering experience.

If you have an income, giving back to God is the most critical line in your budget. Sadly, it is often the first thing to get cut if finances get squeezed. We have given thousands over the years to God through our church, several charities, and even a person in need from time to time. We have never been able to put a price on what God has done and is doing for us. Even in our weakest moments, we easily see how God has always been at work. So we recommend that you have a plan to give back to Him. Prioritize your contribution and charity giving not because you are required to but because you want to give. God gives us forgiveness, mercy, and salvation. Our small contributions build up God's church, enable others to be saved, and meet the needs of the poor around the world. When we look at it that way, we see it as a privilege to give, and never a burden.

> *Each of you should give what you have decided in your heart to give, not reluctantly or under compulsion, for God loves a cheerful giver* (2 Corinthians 9:7).

More real-world advice: if you need to make a large purchase, be careful. Obtain good advice from a person who is financially sound because a misstep can set you back for years. For example, buying a car is necessary in many parts of the world. The ability to get to your workplace or school—well, it has to happen. But think regarding what you need, not what you want. Let the utility of a vehicle drive your decision. In other words, if you need a reliable car to get yourself to work and back, that is understandable. That is also the very type of car you should buy! There is no reason to pay thousands more than you can afford for that truck or nice sports car just because you want it and don't really need it. Plan and follow your budget and consider the total cost of owning a car. You will have the initial purchase price, but then you will need to pay for any taxes, title, plates, and ongoing gas, maintenance, repairs, parking, tolls, and insurance. The cost of ownership is far beyond the purchase price of a vehicle! And this can be a little painful to consider, but generally true: we don't believe purchasing a new car to be a good idea when you are just starting your career. Instead, first consider your job security. If you need to obtain a loan to finance the purchase, you will need to pay that loan regardless of whether you keep your job. And second, driving a new car off a new car lot will decrease its value by 10 to 20 percent the moment you start down the street. (Hard advice to hear, but all car experts know this; it is just fact.) A car is a depreciating asset. In other words, the value of the vehicle continues to decrease as you own it. We strongly encourage you to buy a used car where the payment fits your budget—or better yet, purchase a used car for which you can pay cash.

Be wise in your finances and seek advice. In general, while you're young, it is always good to stick with the principle of obtaining what you need versus what you may want. That said, going to the movie theater or treating a friend to a coffee can be relevant to your week. Having fun is worth a cost. Just be sure to budget for it.

Chapter Seven

JOURNEY ON

By day the Lord went ahead of them in a pillar of cloud to guide them on their way and by night in a pillar of fire to give them light, so that they could travel by day or night. Neither the pillar of cloud by day nor the pillar of fire by night left its place in front of the people (Exodus 13:21, 22).

The Appalachian Trail is symbolic of many paths, both in footsteps and in life. It can be seen as a sort of symbol of your life and the career ahead of you. Just as there were many who prepared the Appalachian Trail decades ago, God continues in His work to make a path for you. You probably feel that you are already on your journey, and that is true. You have a lot to look forward to on your long path ahead.

The Appalachian Trail (AT) officially begins on a mountaintop in northern Georgia. A plaque at that site reads: "Appalachian National Scenic Trail, Springer Mountain, Elevation 3,782 ft." It shows an overview map and details the long trail through fourteen states up through the eastern coast of the United States. Painted on a rock a few yards away is a white rectangular trail marker. Placed in the Chattahoochee National Forest, the southern end of this monumental trail is surrounded by deciduous trees. This secluded nook in the woods is only accessible by foot, and it stands as the official start of the trail for those headed north. There are no iron gates, no blinking lights, no food stands, nothing to draw attention to the trailhead other than a single understated plaque and a nearby white marker. But when facing to the west on the mountaintop, there is a gap through the trees where a hiker can see for miles, perhaps even dream of what lies ahead. We called this chapter Journey On, and the sheer scale and even relative anonymity of the AT are reminiscent of the journey you are on. Life is hard, and it is filled with victories and defeats, challenges, and "vista views" similar to the one a person faces when he or she is at the southern end of the AT. It's up to you how you walk your journey and whether you will walk it dreaming of a life in service of the living God.

The Appalachian Trail has changed little since its early days about one hundred years ago. From those early days on, volunteer groups have worked to improve the path and make it more accessible for hikers. In some cases, they altered the trail route to ease climbs up some of its mountains. There have also been small reroutes made into more attractive wilderness areas, which served to move the trail farther from adjacent roads. Supporters built bridges over waterways and added shelters along the trail for hikers to rest, and they added directional and mileage signs. Many people were needed to complete the work. And because of many political complications, financial challenges, and difficult land acquisitions, it would not be until 2014 that the entire trail was formally acquired and protected by federal or state government agencies. Today the path stretches 2,190 miles from its southern terminus on Springer Mountain all the way to Maine.

Because of its length, it is a massive undertaking to plan a thru-hike, which is hiking the trail in one continuous stretch. Each year, thousands of hopeful nature-seekers plan to take on the challenge. Often known as NOBOs (short for north bounders), most plan to start from the Springer Mountain point and work their way north to Maine. Some, though (yes, they are called SOBOs), begin their trek at the northernmost point and head south. Naturally, there are numerous obstacles along the way. Some hikers fail because of injury, others are not adequately prepared and eventually quit, and some give in to fatigue. Still others have a vision of conquest as they begin, but the daily rigors of hiking a trail over continuous tree roots, rocks, and mud become too much. The cold nights, mosquitoes, or time away from family give pause and wear on the mind. In the end, only one in four who set out to finish the entire thru-hike will complete it. For the victors, the AT gives membership to its prestigious "2,000 Miler Club."[13]

The human spirit required to hike the entire AT is something like that of living a full life in service to God. No one walks the full AT without vision and drive. And no one fills out the life God gave them without a focus on God, a vision for how God can use them, and the drive and resiliency to face the challenges.

Completing the trail is quite a victory, a lifetime achievement, and more than 18,500 hikers have done it. As you can tell, it doesn't happen without planning and foresight. It takes most people five to seven months to complete the trek, so there are strategies to consider in preparation. For instance, timing is critical when coming from either direction. Many NOBOs begin in the early spring because starting later in the year from Georgia will put the finishing hiker in a harsh Maine winter at the north end. Conversely, hiking in the summer heat as one heads south is to be avoided as well.

Of course, the successful thru-hiker needs to prepare physically. The full Appalachian Trail is not a task for the weak. In preparation, the thru-hiker will walk many practice miles with weight on their shoulders, which helps lead to the actual trek. They will practice rock climbing or walk up and down steps in large stadiums to prepare their legs and their minds as well. They wear appropriate footwear to climb mountains, they walk through mud and snow, and they must be prepared to hike over rocks and rough terrain. Those who complete the monster task will tell you that backpack preparedness is essential. The key is having only the necessities at the lightest weight possible. The hiker will carry a tent, sleeping bag, mat, water purification system, water bottles, first aid, extra clothes, food, and, of course, the backpack itself. Ideally, it is recommended to keep that weight at less than 20 percent of the hiker's body weight. (So, if he or she weighs 150 pounds, they should carry no more than thirty extra pounds with them.)

The journey certainly needs training. So does your walk with God! Among other disciplines, persistent Bible study, prayer, and personal ministry will help build your foundation, as we have discussed. Ongoing building of spiritual and other mentoring relationships to support you (as discussed in chapters three and six) are also foundational to your preparation for your life's journey. Training can be difficult and tiring when the person undergoing it doesn't see the point. So keep your eyes focused on the long path forward and serve as an upward call to your peers as you go.

Back to the AT: after that first white trail marker on Springer Mountain, more markers are painted, one after another, on rocks, trees, and posts over the entire 2,190 miles. These simple white markers will guide hikers all the way to Maine. These beacons are a lifeline as the trail twists through lonely, dark wilderness. Your relationship with God is very much like those white indicators, providing clear markers to guide you on your life's journey. You will get lost very quickly on the AT if you ignore the white markers—and you'll get lost quickly in life if you ignore your spiritual relationships.

Leaving Springer Mountain, hikers head generally to the east before turning to the north into the forests of North Carolina. They then trek up through the Great Smokey Mountains National Park and touch the tip of Tennessee. The hiker will make his or her way past daily picturesque vistas and waterfalls. The rugged path of the AT travels over forty-eight mountain peaks that are more than 4,000 feet in elevation![14] The greatest of these and the highest point on the trail is the peak in the Smokies at 6,643 feet (more than one and a quarter miles above sea level). The mountainous terrain often forces a NOBO hiker to walk to the east or west on the way. There are even many trail miles through these forests and mountains that turn to the south in a roundabout way to head north.

Throughout the extended length of the AT, the hiker always needs to take precautions and stay aware of potential dangers. The trail twines through several state and national forests and parks. It's protected land, safe from hunters and therefore home to bears, poisonous snakes, and raccoons among many other wild animals that could cause physical harm or eat the hiker's provisions. There are many signs along the route that remind the hiker to take caution. It is common to come across all types of wildlife, so hikers need to be both knowledgeable and prepared. Since the trail crosses several climate zones, both plants and animals will change. Most plants will be beautiful trees and wildflowers, but the hiker will need to avoid unfriendly patches of poison ivy in the wild, especially in the south. There are more than 250 AT shelters to provide temporary relief from the elements and protect hikers from dangers, and there are AT-focused communities and hostels where individual good Samaritans look to support hikers with food, laundry, and shelter.

As we parallel an AT hiker's journey with your spiritual life journey, remember that God is your shelter, your provider, and your guide when times are challenging, confusing, or just plain hard. Just as the trail itself stays central to a hiker's thoughts, God must be central to your journey.

As the season changes from spring to summer, the NOBO hiker treks through the Blue Ridge Mountains and Shenandoah National Park, continuing through the state of Virginia until they arrive at Harpers Ferry, West Virginia. The historic town known for its early role during the Civil War is the trail's unofficial halfway point. It's also a point in which many will stop their progress and maybe try again another time.

The trail leads north through additional historical parks and across waterfalls and streams. Each state seems to have unique terrain and vegetation. The trail continues through rockier regions, the worst of these being in Pennsylvania, which can severely slow a hiker's progress. From there, the AT leads up through New Jersey and New York as it treks into the New England states and the Green Mountain National Forest in southern Vermont. Then, in the 161 miles of the trail that follows in New Hampshire, primarily through the White Mountain National Forest, the hiker faces climbing seventeen of those forty-eight 4,000-foot mountains along the AT as they near completion.

For the accomplished hiker, the last of the fourteen states is one of the most difficult yet also most rewarding.

The final 282 miles of the Trail leads through Maine and contains some of the most challenging hiking along the entire route. The hardest single mile of the trail is known as the Mahoosuc Notch. It is a steep uphill mountain climb through massive boulders and small crevices that are often wet and dangerous. In this stretch, large animals have been trapped, fallen into the holes of the rock formations, and been unable to escape.

You can imagine that the journey to this point has been an entire spectrum of experiences. There have been sunny days and cloudy days, days of rainfall or snow. Many valleys have followed the many mountain peaks, and a hiker can look back to conquered boulders and stumbling roots. There have been scrapes and burns, snakes and mosquitos, and other creatures as well. As the end nears in late summer for a NOBO, the AT thru-hiker has persevered. He or she has followed the white markers and made daily forward progress with their eyes focused on the end prize.

Life is a lot like this. It seems that, with each passing year, we see more and more how God works with faithful people through both the good and bad. With time, we better understand how God refines character for His glory and purpose. We see His mercy and compassion with faithful dreamers as they persevere.

In northern Maine, the final miles of the trail take the hiker past the shore of the tree-lined Rainbow Lake, which is as beautiful as its name sounds. Grassy Pond is next. This is soon followed by a 4,000-foot climb to the peak of Mount Katahdin in Baxter State Park—to the finale. The Katahdin mountaintop is the highest point in Maine, and hikers feel they can touch the sky. On a clear day, one can see seemingly forever over the sun's reflection and on to distant blue lakes and rivers. This gives pause and deep reflection on the long and often dangerous path that is now behind them. Katahdin means "the greatest mountain" and was named long ago by the Penobscot Indians; it is a fitting end to the Appalachian Trail. There are no trees at the peak. There is some grass and low-growing vegetation, but it's mostly rocks and a cool breeze.

At this last white marker on the trail, there is no award table with people handing out ribbons for a job well done. Any award comes from within. At this peak, there is a mounted plaque stating that the iconic mountain will always be protected and used for public land. A few yards from that plaque, the AT journey officially ends with a brown wooden sign fastened into the rock below. The sign reads: "Katahdin, Baxter Peak, Elevation 5267 ft, Northern Terminus of the Appalachian Trail." And as vast and understated as the AT trail is at its beginning is, so it is at its end.

Spiritually, our lives are much like this. The Bible says our lives are a mist and we must orient ourselves to God's will (James 4:14). Our experience should be one that details walking with God and in which we are in tune with Him and His plan as much as possible. It's not about our glory. It's not about living a smooth, perfect life. It's about walking with Him and being willing to be obedient, a servant, and available for His plans as we make Jesus Lord daily.

YOUR LIFE'S TRAIL

Like the AT, your life's journey will lead you to mountaintops that will cause celebration and into deep valleys that will cause you to pause and grieve. In both career and life, you may find yourself in circumstances in which you travel east, west, or even south in your effort to continue north. Your lengthy hike will require preparation and deliberate planning on your part, but success will really come when you take action. Getting help from others will be a priceless gift on the hard days when you do not feel like persevering. Aiding those around you on your strong days can and will be a priceless gift you offer. Periodically, you will feel you are walking in a dark wilderness with no progress and no end in sight. The hike today looks like the one from yesterday as well as the day before. From time to time you will need to reflect on your map to see how far God has brought you, and hopefully that reflection will bring you joy and more determination. As you progress, there will be dangers to avoid and, at times, shelter required. The opportunities ahead are vast, and there for you to experience, but they require your steps be combined with consistent daily effort.

As we have discussed, you don't have to go at it alone. We started this chapter with an excerpt from Exodus 13, written at a time when God's people were beginning both a spiritual journey in faith and a literal journey on foot. A quick read through surrounding chapters in Exodus provides an impressive story. For the Israelites, all of it must have been an incredibly dramatic experience. For more than four hundred years, the Israelite people in Egypt grew to 600,000 men, and probably more than one million in total (the 600,000 was "besides women and children," Exodus 12:37). They were an enslaved people. There were no vacations to the mountainous regions of the Middle East, no holidays spent on beaches by the sea. At best, they had only heard of experiences outside of Egypt. They were subjugated to this same land for all their lives and had never seen pictures or postcards, nor did they know of any outside sites.

As Moses argued with Pharaoh for the release of his people, the Israelites saw their God protect them against several dreadful experiences. Enslaved for generations, their obedience to God eventually saved them and opened the door to allow them to leave the land. But they did not have white markers laid out for them to point the way. God, in His infinite wisdom, as we saw at the beginning of the chapter, gave them miraculous twenty-four-hour guidance. While they had longed for generations to leave slavery, it was still a scary and tumultuous time. God did not leave them. They in turn were obedient to Him and followed, but with no guarantee that it would be easy. As they left Egypt on foot, the rocky path where God would lead them eventually approached the shores of the Red Sea (Exodus 14). For many of the

Israelites, they had never seen such a body of water! It is hard to imagine. They embarked on a journey like nothing before but still chose to follow their guide.

On the AT, it is wise to follow the white markers regardless of where they lead. Especially on foggy, wet mornings when it is difficult to see where the trail lies, the hiker will make extra effort to stay on the path. The mental and physical preparation the hiker has put in provides him or her with the needed tools to persevere and the determination needed for success when the trail becomes difficult. The NOBO (or SOBO) hiker will need grit to climb the many mountainsides and difficult terrains. They will need to remain obedient to the white markers, even if they turn south (on the NOBO trail) for a time. They follow the markers when it gets hard. And so, at times, must we.

Beyond geographic location, as you launch your life or begin a new career, you will start many new experiences. While you look forward to a promising future, we hope your journey will be uplifting and encouraging. But the reality is that many of the events along the way will be challenging—and often not even make sense. In some circumstances you will not be able to see the purpose or where the future is leading (like fog along the trail). But in your journey, as it is on the AT, and just as it was for the Israelites in Exodus, the importance of your humility and obedience to your guides—God, His Word, and spiritual people in your life—cannot be understated.

The Israelites needed strength of mind and character as they fled Egypt. Their path took them to the shores of the Red Sea with a regretful Pharaoh sending his army to destroy them. It appeared a hopeless situation, an endless sea before them and a vengeful army behind; it seemed like their path had taken a wrong turn. The apparent bad news had traveled fast, and there was a spirit of panic and anxiety in the masses. They couldn't see the way out and, understandably, wanted to return to their captive past. In their view, it was safer where they had lived their lives, as bad as it had been, versus being killed! Despite their loud complaints and shouts to return, the call given them was to remain obedient and humble to God and open their eyes to His plan.

He would not leave them, just as He doesn't leave you.

Under challenging circumstances certain to come, it may be hard for you to remember God's loyalty. Your faithful path will naturally lead to challenges as God continues to shape you. That is the risk of dreaming and moving forward. As discussed in previous chapters, it is often simply easier to remain in the status quo, to not step out on faith, and to not grab hold of your future. Following the dreams that God puts on your heart will lead to new terrain. Exerting deliberate effort toward building a career may provide opportunities that are terrifying. Our strong encouragement is for you to move forward and stay true to your guide, remember your foundation formula, and trust that God has grand plans for you.

At the last minute, when the mass of Israelites could not see a way forward and became convinced there was no way out, they shouted in horror. Pharaoh's army was in hot pursuit and now in sight. As far as the Israelites could see, their path had ended at the shore. It was only then that God opened a clear way for them through the Red Sea. It was a path that only God could have provided at a time when only God could have orchestrated it. God was working to preserve the lives of those He loved. The Almighty rescued the Israelites for the sake of His name so He would not be profaned among the nations (Ezekiel 20:9). He parted the waters for them to gain for Himself everlasting renown (Isaiah 63:12-14, Psalm 106:8). He even placed Pharaoh in leadership to create for Himself the opportunity to display His power so His name would be proclaimed in all the earth (Exodus 9:16). He is profoundly concerned and intimately involved with the lives of those He loves and who He calls to obey His commands. God wants your life and has called you to shine and bring glory to the one who created you in the same way that we have discussed with the many examples in the Bible thus far.

Our next look at a biblical character will show how God moves in one's path through days of celebration and days of sorrow in both life and career. A glimpse into this man's life will provide further strategies to help you excel in the working world and stay faithful to God when your future is cloudy. Think of the biblical heroes we have studied so far. God used Nehemiah, Lydia, and others in their lives and careers to impact the world around them, and we saw the intentional efforts these faithful people put forth in their journeys and how their brand serves as an example for us today. Now it's time to go on a journey with Joseph. A quick read of Genesis chapters 27–50 on your own will be beneficial.

GOD PREPARES JOSEPH

> *Many are the plans in a man's heart, but it is the Lord's purpose that prevails* (Proverbs 19:21).

Joseph's journey is truly applicable for both life and career. His life reflects the proverb above as we see God work—and we see God work through deep human failure. You'll see God's hand come to life through both those who honor God and those who do not know God, all to fulfill a promise.

We discussed in an earlier chapter God's preparation in our lives and how, in His great wisdom, He lays the groundwork for our lives. It is in that spirit that we begin our lesson of Joseph, starting about four thousand years ago in a very different time and culture. For Joseph, the story begins with a conniving grandmother and her son, and through the love story of his mother, Rachel, and his father, Jacob.

Years before Joseph was born, his grandmother Rebekah lived with her husband Isaac in Beersheba, a town just off the coast of the southeastern corner of the Mediterranean Sea. She gave birth to twin boys, naming the oldest Esau and the younger Jacob. Maybe it was because he spent more time at home with Rebekah and was the quieter of the two, or because of the Lord's prophecy to her while still pregnant with the twins, but as both boys grew, Rebekah came to love the younger more than the older (Genesis 25:28). In the prophecy, while she was still pregnant, the Lord told her that her two sons would be divided and the older would serve the younger, who would also be the stronger of the twins (Genesis 25:23). Because Jacob was the favorite child, Rebekah conspired with him and manipulated circumstances in his favor as he grew. There are three separate recorded incidents of their fraudulence in Genesis, and those events would lead to a defining moment for Jacob and set the course for his son Joseph.

To begin with, perhaps in their teen years or shortly after, Jacob came upon a situation that allowed him to take advantage of Esau and connive against his brother for the birthright of the older child. One day, after returning from being away from home for some time, Esau was so hungry that he thought he might die. In his devious thought process, Jacob offered to trade bread and stew to Esau for his birthright. There was no one else to help Esau nearby except for Jacob; Esau did not know where he could find food, or he was too weak to go find it. Esau, in his ignorance and desperation, was more concerned with eating than his birthright, so he made the trade.

Second, sometime later, when the boys were about 40, Esau would marry two Hittite women. Both of these women became a source of frustration for Rebekah. While the Bible is not clear about why, it is probable they did not worship God. Of course, because Jacob was the favored son, any two women with Esau may have found themselves at odds with Rebekah. Regardless, another opportunity presented itself to Rebekah as she overheard Isaac requesting Esau to bring food to him in trade for a special blessing. In a story fitting today's reality television genre, Rebekah conspired with Jacob to deceive her husband. As Isaac was near the end of his life, he was nearly blind when he tried to give his oldest son this special blessing. In a scheme made to take advantage of Isaac's frailty, Rebekah helped Jacob to look, feel, and smell like his older brother. She provided Jacob with food and Esau's clothes. While Isaac suspected something was wrong, he was not able to detect the difference because of his failing eyesight. Through this deception, Isaac gave the special blessing to Jacob in place of Esau. This circumstance, the birthright incident, and maybe others that are unrecorded caused Esau to hold a deep and vengeful grudge against his younger brother, and he vowed to kill Jacob sometime after Isaac's passing.

Upon hearing of Esau's angry vow, the third deception arrives as Rebekah conceives a plan to send her favorite son away. Isaac doesn't seem to know the truth as Rebekah reasons with him in his weak state. To receive his approval, she rages to her husband about Esau's two wives, the Hittite women. Going further, she expresses concern about all the Hittite women and wants Jacob to go to her brother Laban's house to find a wife there. She never mentions the problems between Jacob and Esau, and Isaac consequently gives both his approval and blessing for Jacob to go. Rebekah sends Jacob to Laban to hide him for some time.

Perhaps Jacob would come to regret some of this pretext as he would later be on the receiving end of manipulation and deceit from both Laban and his own children, the latter regarding his son Joseph. But for now, he embarked on a long journey from the land where he had lived his entire life to avoid Esau's vengeance. Laban lived in Harran, located near the modern-day border of Syria and Turkey nearly 400 miles away, toward the northeast corner of the Mediterranean Sea.

One of the greatest qualities of God seen throughout time is the extension of His love and faithfulness to all of us; we are all unqualified receivers. The earth was, and is, filled with family difficulties. Just as with Jacob's family long ago, deception and various schemes exist in households today. It only takes a few minutes of watching the news to find trouble in today's homes. But whether the breakdowns measure in small or large extents, the fact remains that all fall short of God's glory, as Paul wrote in Romans 3. However, the ability of God to work in one's life is not dependent on the perfect righteousness of surrounding family and individuals. For example, many faithful and thriving adults we know today had challenging times when they were younger. They may have come from difficult situations, but they now succeed because of their hard work and obedience to God. In the same way, you may have come from a background that you identify as similar to Jacob's, but that does not preclude you from an amazing future. In fact, as you will soon see in Joseph's story, the very things you may consider a blemish are the things that make you special and unique and may open doors for you in the future. The relational difficulties in Jacob's life were evident at this point, but how that would impact his life and, in turn, his son Joseph, was not. Similar to what it takes to be able to finish the AT, Jacob kept his focus on the mile markers in front of him and remained obedient to God.

Jacob had an incredible dream not long after he left his mother for Harran. As he laid his head on a rock to sleep, he received a direct visit and quite a promise from God despite the sins he had committed and the dysfunction in his family.

> *"I am the Lord, the God of your father Abraham and the God of Isaac. I will give you and your descendants the land on which you are lying. Your descendants will be like the dust of the earth, and you will spread out to the west and to the east, to the north and to the south. All peoples on earth will be blessed through you and your offspring. I am with you and will watch over you wherever you go, and I will bring you back to this land. I will not leave you until I have done what I have promised you"* (Genesis 28:13-15).

Even though he was yet to be married or even meet his eventual wives, God promises Jacob an incredible family line. He also promises that He will always be with Jacob and watch over him. As the sun rose the next morning, Jacob must have had incredible feelings; it seems a direct visit from God would cause the eyes to open wider and the heart to beat a bit faster and more profoundly. Of all the thoughts that may have raced through his head, his recorded response clearly shows deep worshipful gratitude and resolve.

> *Then Jacob made a vow, saying, "If God will be with me and will watch over me on this journey I am taking and will give me food to eat and clothes to wear so that I return safely to my father's house, then the Lord will be my God and this stone that I have set up as a pillar will be God's house, and of all that you give me I will give you a tenth"* (Genesis 28:20-22).

It can be easy to forget that this incredible interchange with God happened during a trip that resulted from deception and lies. This truth is yet another commentary about God using each of us despite ourselves and our dysfunctional families.

The lengthy journey continued for Jacob, and he must have thought of his interchange with God the entire time. When reaching Harran, Jacob found some strangers who knew Laban and his family. While speaking to them, Laban's daughter Rachel happened to walk by while watching sheep. Jacob and Rachel were excited to meet each other, and Rachel ran home to get her father. Laban was thrilled as well to meet Jacob for the first time, and he hugged him. Jacob stayed with his uncle and his family.

Laban had two daughters, the oldest Leah, the younger Rachel. Jacob was smitten with Rachel after just one month of living and working for Laban. He offered to Laban to be his servant for seven years, after which he would be allowed to marry his new love. Laban accepted. As the seven years passed, Jacob must have thought often of Rachel; the Bible says the time passed quickly for him. When the time came to marry Rachel, he was quick to go to Laban to ask for her hand.

They planned a big wedding feast, invited the guests, and prepared the food while music played for the big day. But it must have been very dark that night, somebody had their eyes closed, drinks were tainted, or maybe all parties had covered faces because when Jacob woke the next morning, he found himself lying next to Leah and not Rachel! As it turned out, deception runs in the family. Now Laban had duped Jacob, somehow managing to pull off the marriage of Jacob and Leah, not Jacob and Rachel. Jacob must have thought back to the moment a few years earlier when he misled his father into thinking he was Esau; this time he was on the wrong end of a deceiving scheme. Ironically, showing a character flaw, Jacob immediately questioned Laban about his con, but he had never seemed to question his mother about her schemes years earlier. In the end, in a somewhat fitting taste of his own medicine, Jacob is manipulated by Laban into another seven years of service for the hand of Rachel. After the extended years of service, Laban finally gave his daughter Rachel to Jacob to be his wife.

There continued to be further schemes and deceptions between Laban and Jacob, and at one point a scheme even involved Rachel. Despite being direct relatives, and despite the gracious greeting when they first met, it is hard to imagine how these folks trusted each other at all! In our human thoughts, it's difficult not to wonder if God might have been rethinking his earlier promise to Jacob. But through the imperfections of Jacob and those around him, God continued to work in ways unknown to Isaac's younger son. For Jacob, this time must have felt like an extreme challenge—even hopeless at times. In the big picture, it took fourteen years of persevering service to his father-in-law for him to marry the woman he loved. Think again of the Appalachian Trail. Hikers experience long stretches of challenging and difficult terrain, and many give up. The goal, the dream, is what keeps them going. So it was with Jacob, both as he chose to submit to God and in his pursuit of Rachel.

The marriage culture was different then; it was common for a man to have multiple wives and father multiple children with each. This philosophy had inherent problems, as you might imagine. The relationships would breed envy, and divisions in the clan naturally occurred. As time went on, Jacob fathered at least ten sons and one daughter with his wife Leah and her two servants. Despite the multitude of offspring from those three women, Rachel remained Jacob's favorite wife, but she was yet to give birth to a child. Shamed by the other three mothers, Rachel was jealous of her sister, and bitterness was in both hearts.

Here the story shifts just a bit to Rachel. She often called out to God for a child. It was apparent to her that it was her body that was the problem as her husband bore offspring with the other women. The pain in her soul was likely deep. She may have given up hope at one point or another. But this would prove to be a hole in her heart that God would finally fill. Why God waited so long to bless her was a question she would probably never be able to answer. God finally answered the prayers of Rachel to have a child; Genesis 30:22 records that God listened to her. Jacob's eleventh son was born to Rachel, and she named him Joseph. Naturally, being the first son of his favorite wife and having waited so long for his birth, Jacob loved Joseph most of all his children.

Jacob spent twenty years with Laban, but now it was time to take his wives, their servants, eleven sons, one daughter, and all their animals back to the land from which he had come. But even in the parting from Laban, additional deceptions, lies, and even theft played a big part of the story. Rachel steals her father's idols and later lies to him in a successful attempt to hide them. But after considering all the relational issues that had happened during Jacob's time with him, there was still much good that resulted. At the last moment together, Laban gave his daughters and grandchildren, including a young Joseph, an affectionate kiss goodbye as they left to return to Jacob's homeland.

While on his way, Jacob had his first encounter with Esau in more than two decades since the special blessing incident. Facing a moment he had dreaded for years, Jacob sent a delegation with gifts ahead of him to preempt Esau's vengeance. But there was no need. Esau welcomed Jacob with open arms and a kiss. They wept together, relieved to finally meet again. Esau knew he had plenty of material wealth and didn't want to accept Jacob's gifts. Jacob remembered God's graciousness in his own life and felt as though he had seen God in Esau through the forgiveness that Esau offered. The brothers would peacefully go their way after the encounter.

Like the lion and bear incidents that helped prepare David to face Goliath and later become king, two significant ideals played out in the childhood of Jacob that helped him as he grew into adulthood, and he passed these beliefs on through his children, including Joseph.

1) The belief that God is Almighty.

Throughout the many years of Jacob's life, there are several recorded incidents of sin. Even in the context of sin, Jacob understood God's authority and omnipotence, and this belief was passed on to his children, including Joseph. As Jacob traveled, he built several altars to honor God, and he worshiped at each of these. It was natural to him as he had seen his father worship. Despite his shortcomings and humanness, Jacob was faithful to God. Explicitly told in his youth of the encounters with God that both his father, Isaac, and grandfather, Abraham, had experienced, he learned about God's goodness. His reverence for God was so significant that God continued to carry out His promises through him. One night, in some miraculous way, God wrestled in human form with Jacob until the sun rose for a new day. After Jacob survived the match, God gave him a new name. He would rename him Israel, and he would become the namesake of God's people that we have discussed many times throughout this book: the Israelites.

In keeping with His promise found in Genesis 28, God appeared to Jacob yet another time, reminding him of his new name and the promise of an abundant family.

> *God said to him, "Your name is Jacob, but you will no longer be called Jacob; your name will be Israel. I am God Almighty; be fruitful and increase in number. A nation and community of nations will come from you, and kings will come from your body. The land I gave to Abraham and Isaac I also give to you, and I will give this land to your descendants after you"* (Genesis 35:10-12).

The indelible statement also reminded Jacob of God's might. After another extraordinary moment with God, Jacob—now called Israel—set up another altar and worshiped.

2) It wasn't the picture-perfect family.

We have seen that devious scheming played a significant role in Jacob's life and Joseph's upbringing. We also see the favoritism that Joseph received from his parents, Jacob and Rachel. While there is little mentioned about Joseph's relationships with his siblings or the other wives of Jacob, it is not difficult to think what might have become common in the day-to-day family rhythm. Lying, deception, and favoritism breed dysfunctional families. A little lie here, a manipulation there—these things may have been commonplace. The children would have undoubtedly seen rolled eyes or overheard gossip from one to another or even slanderous comments about their father Jacob. And because Joseph was loved most, there were no doubt favors given to him. Nicer gifts, more loving talk, and more gracious love than the others received from Jacob. These mixed messages no doubt led to competitiveness, jealousy, and hatred.

Sometime later, Jacob's favored wife passed away while giving birth to the last of his twelve sons. It seems that while they were traveling, Rachel went into difficult labor and, after giving birth to her second son, who would be named Benjamin, died almost immediately. Israel lost his love, and Joseph lost his mother. Perhaps within the hearts of this troubled family, Leah and the two servants even found clandestine delight that Rachel was no longer in their midst.

To summarize, Joseph grew up in a cloud of dysfunction, including: the loss of his biological mother, stepsiblings who were jealous and hated him, stepmothers who also likely resented and possibly even hated him, and just a general culture of deceit and manipulation that ran deep within his family. If you have grown up with dysfunction like any of this, you know how difficult it is to see God's sovereignty when family life is so difficult. Joseph's life had many challenges from this point forward. His past, his family, and his circumstances provided him the opportunity to go to God, trust God, and surrender his strife-filled family to God. Ultimately, all this dysfunction was in service of God's plan for the Israelites, which is incredible. God uses all challenges for His glory if we follow Him and stay faithful like Jacob and Joseph.

TEN LESSONS FROM JOSEPH

For Joseph, there were deep roots of resentment that started with the three other mothers well before he was born and carried on through his childhood. We see it more plainly in Genesis 37 when Joseph was just 17. Among other favors he received, Joseph was given a special robe that his father made to show he was loved the most. He wore it often in the sight of the rest of the family, perhaps to exploit the favoritism, or maybe because he liked it so much, or both. Whatever the case, imagine the lifetime of resentment the brothers had built up through being lesser-loved children. Joseph and his brothers had a long way to go before they would ever be unified as a family that served God. These ten lessons from Joseph's life will shine some light on the things that were required for that to happen.

1) Persevere through your past, and take what is good into your future.

Give thanks to the Lord, for he is good (Psalm 136:1).

As we go forward into Joseph's journey, we see at least two positive ideals that he took from his upbringing. One: he chose to be devoted to God in all circumstances. Two: he decided to keep loving his family despite his and their shortcomings. He could have made other choices, especially as he would face vigorous character tests in both areas. Joseph sets an example for us in finding peace and goodness with God and family when it's hard. Given the trials he would face, we doubt he had to make those choices just once. It's often said that forgiveness is a journey, not a destination. As it has been for us and will be for you, decisions like these will need to be made repeatedly as our enemy continues to fight against us throughout our lives.

One night, Joseph had a dream that started a litany of unforeseen changes in the family dynamic. He dreamed about his brothers humbling themselves before him. It's unknown whether he detailed the vision in a simple descriptive manner or if Joseph told it in a prideful, aggressive way. But as anyone could imagine, Joseph's dream about his brothers bowing before him did not sit well with them. The brothers had had enough of this young man. Sometime shortly after, the brothers were away from home tending to their sheep. Joseph was with his father and perhaps not out in the fields keeping sheep because of his higher honor, which would have naturally rubbed the wounds even deeper. Putting him in a role that would place him somewhat superior to the brothers, Israel sent Joseph to check on the brothers and see if they were well. Everything changed from that moment on.

They may have discussed the possibility before this moment, and they certainly discussed their disdain toward Joseph. Perhaps they had talked the night before of the inherent struggles and even jealousness they felt, and the discussion escalated to antagonism and unforgiving rage. Regardless, the anger was at the forefront of the brothers' minds as Joseph approached from a distance—wearing his special robe. They were about twenty-five miles from their father, so if they agreed to keep it to themselves, no one would know about their intended murder. Their hatred was immense, for in their plan the brothers would not quickly kill Joseph and bury him. Instead, they chose to let him suffer in a deep hole in the ground, one symbolic of the hole in their hearts.

It must have felt like the end for Joseph, the teenager. The bigger, stronger brothers worked together as some tied him up and threw Joseph into a cistern while others kept a lookout and a few others tended the sheep. Joseph possibly yelled in rage or fear, but they probably tied his hands and wrapped his mouth so no one would hear him. In a matter of minutes, Joseph went from being the premier child of the household to now being abandoned in a literal pit of despair. The horrific incident intensified Joseph's journey through his challenging family relationships, taking him to a place in which he could have turned to, or turned away from, God.

2) "Pit" days will come.

> *How long, O Lord? Will you forget me forever? How long will you hide your face from me? How long must I wrestle with my thoughts and day after day have sorrow in my heart?* (Psalm 13:1, 2).

Like Joseph, and just like the Appalachian Trail, you will have peaks and valleys as you launch both your life and career. Perhaps David felt like Joseph in his pit of despair when he wrote the beginning of Psalm 13 (above). If you've experienced it, you know that graduation from high school or university can bring great joy and a victorious feeling of accomplishment. Landing your first job in your field of choice will also bring gladness. There will be other heights as well, and hopefully a lot of them. But your life can easily take downward turns due to certain tragedies or simply from poor choices. You may have already experienced deep challenges and difficulties. And while the enemy tempts you with feelings of God forgetting you, as David suffered at the beginning of Psalm 13, cornering those thoughts and resolving to trust God is what we implore you to do. Take a look at how David does just that by the end of Psalm 13.

> *But I trust in your unfailing love; my heart rejoices in your salvation. I will sing to the Lord, for he has been good to me* (Psalm 13:5, 6).

Trusting God as Joseph did, during the hardest of times, is imperative to staying faithful for the rest of our lives. When Joseph was beaten, thrown down a well, and nearly murdered by his brothers, then sold as a slave, falsely imprisoned, forgotten, and forsaken by man—deep in his heart, he still trusted God. He is a beautiful example of faith persevering through adversity. God was always with Joseph, molding him into who he was through his trials. How much more do we need to be molded to bring God glory? Joseph's life is a timeline of what perseverance and trust can look like in our daily lives.

We (Phil and Beth) have both had unexpected "pit" moments in our careers. Beth landed her dream job with her dream company before she graduated from university. All was well. But as a new hire working with other seasoned employees, negative aspects of her character were exposed. Within five years, her mixed performance was neither good enough to be promoted nor was she at the point of being fired. This warning left her in the space of figuring out how to change, trust God, and let God lead. Contrary to Beth's quick acquisition of her dream job after college, it took Phil three post-graduate years of temporary and contract work, project work that ended at the project completion, or embarrassing times of unemployment to finally break through to what he considered his first career job. Through no fault of his own, he was laid off from employment three times during those years. It provided sleepless nights, questioning the future, insecurity, and at times stress on our new marriage. For both of us, these "professional pits" required grit, perseverance, and seeking God's will. In both cases, we can see how God worked through the challenges, but it took years of working through emotional, financial, and character challenges to overcome and see God always at work.

Sometimes circumstances outside of us are entirely beyond our control. However, God can reveal things that are within your power so you can pull yourself out of a pit. These things can include: going after character change after a rough piece of performance feedback; taking on professional training and development if skills are lacking; or pivoting to a new job that is a better match in a time of performance issues. You have control over your morale, your appearance, your attitude, and your performance. At other times, however, you can and will be at the complete mercy of others and their choices. You may be called on by God to wait, to persevere, and to learn lessons of love and humility when it is extremely hard. In all of the cases we wrote about above, we grew in the professional pits God allowed. You will too.

Joseph found himself in a moment of surrender at the bottom of his pit. He was not able to pull himself out of the cistern, and if not for a couple of the brothers sharing a troubled conscience, the group would have left him for dead. As it was, they chose to fake his death by pulling him from the pit and selling him as a slave to passing merchants headed to Egypt. Despite the ugliest of days for Joseph, the Almighty God whom he had grown to revere was always at work.

Despite God's plan, it is hard to believe that Joseph was relaxed and merely trusting in God as the merchants took him away in chains. Purchased for some silver like a piece of clothing, if there had been any previous question, he now understood the depth of his brothers' resentment and hatred. As far as Joseph knew, he would likely never see his father again, and he knew his brothers would devise a lie to explain his disappearance.

The merchants took him more than 300 miles away to Egypt, a place Joseph may have heard about but had likely never seen. It was a long trip. Joseph likely felt a tremendous mix of emotions on this journey: gratitude for being alive, grief at the loss of his family, anger against his brothers, anxiety for his future. His life was not straightforward. His family had let him down. His task now was to find a way to move forward with God into his new life. The merchants took him to the largest city he had surely ever seen, and then resold him to Potiphar, a high-level government official who worked in the role of overseeing the royal prison. Imagine yourself in Joseph's shoes for a moment. Appreciate the faith he would need to muster any desire to serve God faithfully through these traumatic experiences.

3) Let your life show your gratefulness to God, not just your lips.

> *I will exalt you, O Lord, for you lifted me out of the depths and did not let my enemies gloat over me. O Lord my God, I called to you for help and you healed me. O Lord, you brought me up from the grave; you spared me from going down into the pit. Sing to the Lord, you saints of his; praise his holy name* (Psalm 30:1-4).

In chapter five, we discussed working as if working for Jesus Himself. Joseph seems to have that heart as we read Genesis 39. It could have been that Joseph saw his only way out of being a slave was to be the best one he could be, or maybe he feared for his life, or perhaps it was just a pure heart to work hard in gratefulness because he saw that God had saved his life through the pit incident. Maybe he just trusted that God was going to make something great, and to His glory, out of all this, or perhaps it was a combination of all of these. Regardless, his impact on those who saw him work was striking, especially to Potiphar himself.

> *The Lord was with Joseph and he prospered, and he lived in the house of his Egyptian master. When his master saw that the Lord was with him and that the Lord gave him success in everything that*

he did, Joseph found favor in his eyes and became his attendant. Potiphar put him in charge of his household, and he entrusted to his care everything he owned . . .

So he left in Joseph's care everything he had; with Joseph in charge, he did not concern himself with anything except the food he ate (Genesis 39:2-4, 6).

Imagine being such a solid employee that your boss totally trusts you will take care of everything that is needed, and that he or she only needs to be concerned about what is for dinner! Joseph was that guy. He was at the mercy of Potiphar as a slave, but he sincerely believed in respecting his Almighty God. That is what drove him. He was able to look past his misfortune and focus on two things: working diligently and worshiping God. Joseph was actually sharing his faith with a high-achieving man who did not know God. And yet it was Joseph's beliefs and work ethic that made the difference. This ethic is extremely applicable today. His faith was communicated by the Joseph Brand—how he worked and by his character. The consistency of his character and faith in God transcended his circumstances.

From his low pit moment at the hands of his brothers, Joseph was now at another pinnacle point in his life and career. There was no way, however, Joseph could have been prepared for his next valley—and it would be a low one. Perhaps Potiphar's wife had made suggestive hints to Joseph a few times earlier, or possibly she just talked about her declining marriage. Maybe she winked at Joseph while giving him a devilish eye and ran her fingers through her hair to flirt with the handsome slave. Either way, Joseph was working daily in their house, and Potiphar's wife was bold in her wish to have sex with him, clearly crossing the line of marriage morality. Joseph knew his limits and could not have imagined breaking his trust with Potiphar and, more so, his Almighty God. He repeatedly resisted her by focusing on his work. One day he made a mistake, however, by being alone in the house with Potiphar's wife.

Hoping yet again to snag him to her bed, she found him and reached for him with no one around, and she actually tore some of his clothing away. The level to which Joseph was personally tempted by his interactions with the wife is not clear, but in this instant, he literally ran from his temptation, perhaps now regretting having left himself in the home alone with her. The wife then lied to Potiphar, turning the tables and telling him Joseph had been the aggressor. It was a believable story since she held Joseph's garment in her hand. Understandably, Potiphar was livid because he had entrusted so much to Joseph. And now he believed Joseph had tried to take advantage of his wife. Without hesitation and without discussion, Potiphar quickly threw Joseph in prison.

4) Always take the high road, the road of integrity.

> *I know that you are pleased with me, for my enemy does not triumph over me. In my integrity you uphold me and set me in your presence forever* (Psalm 41:11, 12).

Joseph had been at the wrong end of lying schemes before. He had seen it often in his family, so this was really nothing new. The most recent had been that literal pit, but there were likely many others throughout his childhood. This situation must have hurt his soul, however, as it was an attack on his character as much as it was an attack from the wife. Yet his clear conscience gave him peace. He knew that except for the mistake of being alone with Potiphar's wife, he had taken the high road and resisted sinning against both Potiphar and God.

The lesson is more than just resisting sin, though that is an excellent point of the story as well. Taking the high road, or the path of integrity, will mean that you must be honest when you are not meeting expectations on a project, or when you are tempted to lie; and that you will do each task at your work the best you can whether someone is watching or not. It means you will live as a higher call to those around you whether you are doing simple tasks or something more challenging. Integrity is not being a gossip or slandering your coworker. It is about doing what is right and showing strong character in the face of wrong.

And while there may be momentary setbacks, keep in mind that God sees you just as Psalm 41 (above) suggests.

The life and career of Joseph had taken another major downfall, but this one was through entirely no fault of his own. It seems this experience was another pit moment, one that, this time, God had prepared him for. He had learned before to rely on God in injustice, in deceit, and in disappointment, but perhaps in God's eyes he needed another, deeper lesson. Joseph's view was that God had saved him and God was Almighty, and he continued to worship and hold God in high honor instead of blaming God for all the bad that had happened. But now he was being thrown into prison, and as the shackles clinked together and other prisoners likely mocked and laughed at him, Joseph fought to remain hopeful. And in another incredible example of good character, Joseph does not seem to lash out, but instead keeps his focus on being righteous.

> *While Joseph was there in prison, the Lord was with him; he showed him kindness and granted him favor in the eyes of the prison warden. So the warden put Joseph in charge of all those held in the prison, and he was made responsible for all that was done there. The warden paid no attention to anything under Joseph's care, because the Lord was with Joseph and gave him success in whatever he did* (Genesis 39:20-23).

5) Life isn't fair, but you can still shine.

> *In God, whose word I praise, in the Lord, whose word I praise, in God I trust; I will not be afraid. What can man do to me?* (Psalm 56:10, 11)

David wrote this psalm at a hard moment; he had been taken captive by his warring enemies. He seems to remind himself of God's faithfulness and stronghold in moments of adversity. Likewise, there will be times ahead for you that will be stumbling blocks: financial struggles, the loss of a job, health issues, or challenging family relationships. Some setbacks will feel more personal than others. Like the deceit of Potiphar's wife, you may find someone taking credit for a successful project you achieved, or you might hear of someone lying about you to their advantage. Coworkers or "friends" may lie to you or about you. Those things have all happened to us and are mostly out of your control. What you can control, however, is your spirit and resolve in response. Being on the wrong end of these situations is difficult and takes much prayer and resolve. It helps to remember the foundation formula (chapter three) and always consider how God is shaping you. Focus on the long path ahead on your journey and think of stumbling blocks like these as temporary setbacks.

The Joseph Brand was remarkable and consistent. It is astonishing to read the thoughts of the prison warden at the end of Genesis 39 and compare them to the opinions of Potiphar near the beginning of the same chapter. Their comments are nearly identical and speak volumes about Joseph's character and desire to honor God. It would have been understandable for prison work to have sapped his spirit, at least a little, but it did not. After all, he did nothing wrong and was only there because someone had lied about him. Similarly, you may find yourself on a career path or in a job you do not like, or one that is not a great fit. Most everyone experiences this at some point. Maybe the job is too challenging, or perhaps it is not challenging enough. Perhaps the boss is not that kind. Or perhaps you are having a difficult time even finding a job and have struck out in multiple interviews. Let Joseph be your character model regardless of your circumstance.

What follows later for Joseph is an interesting interchange with fellow prisoners with whom he had become friends while taking care of them. The two men known only by their job titles—cupbearer and baker—had deeply offended Pharaoh, the king of Egypt. They angered the Egyptian king so much that he sent them to the prison where Joseph was already serving.

While we are not sure what Joseph's duties were as he oversaw some of the prison operations, it is conceivable there was a good amount of time to do nothing but sit and talk to one's neighbor. While the cupbearer and baker seemed to have been previously acquainted, Joseph was probably a new relationship for them. Part of his earlier success working for Potiphar and now in prison was due to his genuine concern for the people around him. Joseph made people feel he cared, and that empathy did not change while he was in prison.

One morning in prison, Joseph noticed there was something wrong with both of these men simply by seeing the looks on their faces. He was concerned enough to ask what they were feeling. They each had worrisome dreams the night before but didn't have a clue to their meaning. Joseph, knowing it was not him but God working in him, offered to help. The cupbearer told Joseph his dream, and, as it turned out, Joseph correctly interpreted it. The dream was about his release from prison in just three days and that he would be returned to his previous position. The baker was so encouraged about the cupbearer's dream that he eagerly asked Joseph about his dream as well. Unfortunately, his vision was not a good one. In fact, it was horrible news for the baker. Joseph told him his dream meant he would be dead in three days. Joseph's interpretations of both dreams were correct. Despite the mixed emotions involved, Joseph once again rose to the occasion to show empathy, honesty, and true friendship.

6) Be willing to take part in hard conversations.

> *May integrity and uprightness protect me, because my hope is in you* (Psalm 25:21).

Joseph sets another example for us here, in Genesis 40, and it applies to relationships with classmates, coworkers, family, and friends. If you love God, being truthful in most situations is not that difficult. But from time to time, the hard truths must be told as well. We offer the psalm above to underscore and emphasize this idea. Your hope and security should be in God, not in the desire to have others think highly of you.

Being willing to give and receive hard truths are both needed skill sets for successful careers and authentic relationships. Your response when your boss expresses disappointment in your performance should be humble and accepting, not blaming or denying. Throughout God's Word, and even in the workplace today, balancing empathy and humility in challenging conversations is one key to success. And, like Joseph, keep your eyes open to those who may be having trouble. God will open doors for you to show your true Christianity away from the church worship services. Look for those times and be the example Joseph is here. Joseph showed in his actions and character that the Lord was with him. It was evident to others. Can the same be said of us in the workplace?

Joseph explained his full story to the cupbearer. He told him how his brothers had sold him off and how he came to Egypt via the merchants. And he told him the story of the situation with Potiphar's wife that landed him in prison. In return for giving the cupbearer the good news of his dream, Joseph only asked that he help him get out of prison. But regardless of his intentions or his initial dismay over hearing about Joseph's situation, when the cupbearer left prison he forgot about Joseph and their relationship—and did nothing.

Joseph sat in prison for two long, additional years after the cupbearer forgot him. It certainly provided him time to reflect, and his thoughts must have journeyed along a trail of anger and frustration to trust and resolve. He would probably see other prisoners come and go as he continued his work for the warden. Joseph's career had plummeted with this undeserving demotion. Across his entire life, he must have felt, it was unclear whether God had any plans to bless him at all. Maybe he tried to make sense of the dream about the brothers bowing to him. Or maybe he struggled in his mind, once again, with being sold off by his brothers because of their hatred. Maybe he replayed the tape in his mind around Potiphar and Potiphar's wife and the injustice of that circumstance.

The bridges Joseph had crossed to that point must not have seemed straightforward, nor was God's will clear to him. He had no choice but to sit and wait on God. Joseph continued to choose to lean on the hugeness of God. After all, he likely reminded himself often, he did believe in an Almighty God. He must have learned that God was trustworthy, all-knowing, faithful, and righteous. Like Abraham, Joseph resolved that, despite not understanding why God allowed terrible things to happen, he would believe and persevere. We often struggle to understand suffering and seek meaning from pain. In the end, Joseph still trusted. There is so much we learn from his faith.

7) Take time for self-assessment.

> *Search me, O God, and know my heart; test me and know my anxious thoughts. See if there is any offensive way in me and lead me to the way everlasting* (Psalm 139:23, 24).

Just as David asked God to search his ways, a big part of being intentional and growing in your life and career is taking the time to assess your progress and future planning. It's important to take the time needed to look back and see how God has moved, what skills you have learned, and what impact you have made. Prioritizing this time can also assist in the bigger picture when the future ahead seems foggy, when you can't see why things are happening. Make notes you can reflect on in the future and create a list of your accomplishments. You'll find that doing these self-driven periodic assessments every six months or so will help lead you to deliberate action and contribute to building your career, developing your aspirations, and being intentional about how you want to grow in the life you lead for God. The journaling and assessment work in our corresponding *Action Planner* can get you started in these areas as well.

Having authentic and vulnerable relationships in your life also will be extremely helpful with this. Other people are likely going to be better at objectively answering questions about your impact. We don't always have a proper perspective on ourselves, so having others to talk to about our growth and our plans is imperative. Your close friends in the church, coworkers at the office, and mentors all can be of huge help here. Joseph allowed himself to grow through circumstances even when the conditions were not ideal. This choice of attitude is evident as we look at the next chapter in his life.

Pharaoh, of course, as king of Egypt, ranked higher in position than Potiphar. He was a busy man who had plenty of officials, servants, and leaders who worked under him to oversee the country. One evening Pharaoh laid down to sleep and had a rough night. He had two vivid dreams that night, waking up multiple times as he found himself deeply troubled. The first dream was of seven fat cows and seven skinny cows. The second was about seven healthy heads of grain and seven burnt heads of grain. When he awoke in the morning, he immediately called for help by meeting with the best magicians and wise men to help him interpret the dreams. They quickly came, and the group included the previously imprisoned cupbearer. They must have looked at each other quizzically as Pharaoh explained his nighttime visions. A few may have thrown out some thoughts about the dreams, but others likely discounted them quickly, and no one dared tell outright lies to Pharaoh.

At that moment the cupbearer remembered the man who befriended him in prison, and the cupbearer spoke up. He told Pharaoh about Joseph's interpretation of his dream while in prison and how things played out precisely as Joseph had said. When Pharaoh inquired further, they discovered that this man was still in prison. The king immediately sent for Joseph.

These events illustrate that the course of our journey can change in an instant, and we should always be prepared to see God work. As far as Joseph knew, the sun rose early that morning, like most days, and this day was going to be like all the others in recent years. He may have been thinking about cleaning the cells, feeding fellow prisoners, and eventually sleeping in his cell again as the sun set later that evening. Joseph didn't know about the dreams Pharaoh had experienced during the night, nor did he know about the meeting of Pharaoh and all his dream interpreters. Joseph probably had scraggly hair and an untrimmed beard. He smelled, and his clothes likely reeked of sweat and body odors as well. But all of that was about to change. Joseph was told he was being summoned. He was cleaned, shaved, given new clothes, and brought before the king.

Confident that the Almighty God was with him, he stood silently before Pharaoh as the others looked on. The cupbearer was hoping that Joseph, now 30 years of age, would have answers that would please his king. Pharaoh began explaining the vision of the cows and grain to Joseph. He was probably unsure whether this prisoner was going to be helpful, but he was also likely in a bit of panic as those he trusted had been unhelpful.

Crediting God's insight as God revealed it, Joseph confidently understood the dreams. As it was with the cupbearer and the baker, Joseph had good news and bad news for Pharaoh. The good news of the fat cows and good grain meant the next seven years would be bountiful. This answer was encouraging and well received. Those standing with Pharaoh smiled and probably applauded as that part of the dream was clear. But again, Joseph did not mince the bad news; he understood that thoroughness in his explanation was imperative. He went on to say that the skinny cows and burnt grain would mean seven years of harsh famine would follow the bountiful years. The response left the room silenced. Joseph was prepared for this moment, for both the good and the bad. He saw so much of this in his life and, ultimately, trusted in the power of Almighty God. He grew to this place of influence from just 17 to 30 years of age, and he did so by being in touch with God and himself. He had reached a point in which he could interpret and discuss the dreams in a way that Pharaoh would listen and act.

8) Grow your resume by building skill sets and experiences.

> *Create in me a pure heart, O God, and renew a steadfast spirit within me* (Psalm 51:10).

David saw and experienced an ugly side of his soul. In his prayerful response to God in Psalm 51 after the exposed murder and adultery in his life, we see him calling out to God. He asks for a renewed spirit, and that God would create in him a pure heart. Imagine if you were going to pray these very words to God for yourself. You would likely not expect these qualities to show up the next day. Change is a process. As we've discussed in earlier chapters, God is always at work in your world shaping you and helping you grow. Whether it is the softness of your heart or a specific skill set God has given you that will help you grow your resume and character—or all of these things—it takes consistent and deliberate effort to achieve personal growth.

Among many others, a unique skill set God created in Joseph was the ability to understand people, lead people, and display insights into their dreams and lives. These were skills Joseph had when he was younger, and he continued to develop them as he grew. It started with his own family as a teenager. He kept growing in these areas in his early twenties with Potiphar, and then with the prison warden later in his mid-twenties. His continued development then provided an opportunity to help the cupbearer and baker, and later his skills unlocked the way for him to be helpful and effective with Pharaoh. Had Joseph sat silently and done nothing with this gift from God, or given into resentment, bitterness, hatred, or other sins, the door before him simply would not have opened.

Pharaoh had asked for someone to interpret his dreams. In today's career terms, Pharaoh was looking to fill a project opportunity role. Again, the unique skills Joseph had developed and was continuing to improve opened this door. Not only did he fill the request, he went beyond expectations. Based on Joseph's work on this project, the Egyptian leadership now had a new problem statement. How would Egypt survive during the seven-year famine to come? Joseph already had an answer; he was ready to move beyond what Pharaoh had asked. Perhaps it was this kind of thinking that caused Potiphar (earlier) and the prison warden to like and trust him so much.

Joseph relayed some practical insights and suggested a plan to Pharaoh and the other officials. They would collect and store a good portion of the grain harvested over the bountiful years and use it during the barren years to follow. Pharaoh was so impressed and relieved from this interaction with Joseph that a massive promotion followed. It would prove to be more than Joseph ever expected or hoped. Pharaoh placed Joseph second in command over all of Egypt and had him report directly to him. Joseph simply had the right resume, the right skills, and the exemplary character needed at the right time to be called upon for this job. He had honed that resume for more than a decade for this moment.

> *So Pharaoh said to Joseph, "I hereby put you in charge of the whole land of Egypt." Then Pharaoh took his signet ring from his finger and put it on Joseph's finger. He dressed him in robes of fine linen and put a gold chain around his neck. He had him ride in a chariot as his second-in-command, and men shouted before him, "Make way!" Thus he put him in charge of the whole land of Egypt* (Genesis 41:41-43).

Joseph traveled the country in his chariot as the "fat cow" years played out. The bounty gathered during those years far exceeded expectations, and the collection of food was so plentiful that Joseph didn't keep track of the surplus. These were remarkably productive years for Egypt; there was plenty of food for all. But, as foretold, the "skinny cow" years followed. Beyond what Joseph said, not only did Egypt experience famine, the famine spread throughout the world. And guess who had food to sell to peoples scattered in various nations? First it was the Egyptians who came to purchase grain for their families, and they were followed by people from surrounding countries who came to make purchases. The demand was high, and the price and profits must have pleased Pharaoh. Joseph was a golden employee.

9) If you keep your eyes open for opportunities, they will come.

> *But now, Lord, what do I look for? My hope is in you* (Psalm 39:7).

If Joseph had been a NOBO hiker on the AT, his journey to this point would have involved both beautiful vista heights and dark rocky valleys. Having taken a path with far more misdirection than he ever would have expected, his trail took him east, west, and south in his efforts to trek north. You will find that your career will likely be similar. Like the AT, and like checkers on a checkerboard, your career over time will move forward, laterally, backward, and forward again. The story of Joseph gives us a view of how things may look. Your valleys may be deeper than expected, and the heights better than deserved. Joseph stayed the course with God and kept moving forward where he could while looking for opportunity. Any forward motion in prison must have seemed minimal at best. Maybe he hoped that the conversations he had there would at least bring some benefit to others or himself. Perhaps he counted on his times of prayer to get through the hard emotions and betrayals, or maybe he simply allowed Almighty God to work on his heart until the time when he was ready for the big jump. Regardless of the direction you feel your career (or life for that matter) is headed, remain close to God, continue to develop your skills, and keep your eyes open. He will show you your path.

For Joseph, however, was this the pinnacle? Although now a distant memory from twenty years earlier, there was still the unanswered dream of his brothers bowing before him. He may have thought that this was it, the peak, given that he now had the high position of authority of which he had dreamed. He may have assumed he would never see his family again. But Israel and the brothers found themselves in the same predicament as the rest of the world around them. They were in desperate need of grain, and they heard there was plenty to be purchased in Egypt.

Ten of the brothers went to Egypt as instructed by their father, leaving only the youngest, Benjamin, at home. The family was in desperate need as so many were by this time. Being from a foreign land, perhaps they were sent to someone as high as Joseph before they could be approved to purchase grain. As they approached Joseph, they stopped and bowed to him, just as the dream had predicted so many years ago. Somehow, Joseph was able to keep his mixed emotions in check. He immediately recognized his brothers from more than twenty years earlier. The brothers, thinking Joseph was dead or long gone, had no idea of the Egyptian minister who stood before them.

Joseph had been somewhat hardened, was now careful to assess, and had grown to be somewhat shrewd. The memories of being mistreated by his brothers and their mothers were not forgotten. They had lied to his face and lied about him to others as well. They had sold him off to strangers, stopping just short of murder. They didn't like him; they never had. In addition to his family, lying Potiphar's wife and the forgetful cupbearer were at least two others who caused him severe suffering. For his meeting with the brothers, and knowing their devious past, Joseph had in mind an orchestrated response that was designed to check their intentions and perhaps repay a portion of the pain they had caused him.

In his test, he spoke to them harshly, wondering who they were and if their father was still alive. While hiding his identity, he spoke to them in the authoritative voice of a government official, and he asked about his younger brother, who was born when his mother died. In what may have been a satisfying moment, he put the brothers in prison for three days, calling them spies. For an exchange of silver, Joseph granted them grain and let nine of them go back home, keeping one in prison until they could bring the youngest to Joseph. But he wasn't finished. He secretly placed the previously exchanged silver back in their sacks. Later, the brothers' discovery of the silver convinced them they had just sealed their death sentence. They were confident they would be hunted and killed for stealing from the Pharaoh's second-in-command.

They told their father Jacob all that had happened, worried about what was going to happen next, and felt frightened to return to Egypt. They argued with their father over what to do. They had to return to obtain the release of their captured brother, Simeon, but uncertainty brought painful memories of his lost favorite son, and this caused Israel to hesitate to send his youngest. But the brothers were right that they had to go, so they readied their return. In an offer of penance, they doubled the amount of silver and added the best of other products to help trade for additional grain. This time, Benjamin traveled with them, and they were on their way.

Painful memories may fade, but they rarely go away completely. As the brothers returned to Joseph, he reunited with all of them, pulling Simeon from prison to join them. All twelve were reunited for the first time since before the pit incident, including Benjamin, with whom he shared a mother. Now a grown man, Benjamin had been just a child when Joseph last saw him. Joseph missed growing up with him, doing things like wrestling in the fields or tending sheep together. His memories went back to his teen years when he anticipated being the big brother and dreaming of all the fun they would have. All of that, however, had been eliminated at the hand of the other brothers. The emotion of seeing Benjamin and thinking of time lost was too much for Joseph, and he dashed from the room to weep privately.

Joseph tested his brothers' intentions further, and there were more tears until the inevitable moment. Joseph cleared the room of all others, leaving only himself and the eleven with him. By now, still in the midst of the harsh famine, Joseph was seeing more clearly what God had done through all these years.

> *Then Joseph said to his brothers, "Come close to me." When they had done so, he said, "I am your brother Joseph, the one you sold into Egypt! And now, do not be distressed and do not be angry with yourselves for selling me here, because it was to save lives that God sent me ahead of you. For two years now there has been famine in the land, and for the next five years there will not be plowing and reaping. But God sent me ahead of you to preserve for you a remnant on earth and to save your lives by a great deliverance. So then, it was not you who sent me here, but God . . .*
>
> *"You shall live in the region of Goshen and be near me—you, your children and grandchildren, your flocks and herds, and all you have. I will provide for you there, because five years of famine are still to come. Otherwise you and your household and all who belong to you will become destitute (Genesis 45:4-8, 10, 11).*

Their faces looked stunned, and their minds were terrified as Joseph spoke. But the fog finally lifted from Joseph's journey as the reasons for the past were revealed for a greater future purpose. It was to preserve the family line and thus the promise of Almighty God.

After more convincing, tears, and hugs, the brothers left to retrieve their father and families. Israel would need to be convinced as well, and understandably so. Having his son found alive was one thing, but the tale of what God had done, where he had taken him, and the reasons why were almost too much to fathom. But Israel was convinced (through a dream), and the whole family packed up and moved its belongings to Egypt.

The reunion with his father was as emotional as we might think. Israel was once again able to hug his favorite son. They wept together as the rest of his family, the Israelites, looked on. Joseph introduced them to Pharaoh. And it was at Pharaoh's direction that Joseph had the family settle in the best land in Egypt. In time the family, saved from the severe famine, continued to multiply.

Opportunity comes as we surrender to God, trust in God, and grow in God. It took twenty years for this to play out for Joseph—years that included so much injustice and rejection. How much more do we need to stay faithful and allow ourselves to be led by God as we diligently grow in our lives?

10) You'll never go wrong with love and humility.

> *He guides the humble in what is right and teaches them his way. All the ways of the Lord are loving and faithful toward those who keep the demands of his covenant* (Psalm 25: 9, 10).

Joseph could have reacted much differently in these turbulent scenarios. Imagine the first sighting, the shock, and the returned memories that must have flooded his mind in an instant as his brothers walked up to him. He could have run away, reacted in anger, or even turned to violence. Any of those reactions would have been understandable. He had experienced multiple "surprise moments" before. But this moment was deep-rooted, close to his heart, and the biggest test he had ever faced. It returned his thoughts to his childhood—specifically to "the pit." If he had reacted out of hatred or revenge, the story would have gone differently and cast a shadow over all he had accomplished. By this time, however, Joseph had learned to follow God's lead.

As this psalm suggests, resolving to let God lead by having a humble heart will teach you the ways of God. God may have surprises for you as well. Whether it is an encouraging promotion, discouraging removal from a project, or a flash of bad memories from the past, as it was for Joseph, reacting with love and humility is always appropriate and righteous. You cannot make a bad choice with humility and love.

From the high of being the favorite teenager to the position of a lowly slave, to being Potiphar's top guy, to being jailed and forgotten, to being called to answer a question, and on to being named as the right hand of Pharaoh, Joseph's checkerboard career rose to heights that only God could direct. His life's journey played out according to God's plan at God's direction. God was there at his pit. He was there when Potiphar thought so highly of Joseph. God was present when Potiphar's wife lied. He was in prison when the warden was so pleased. He was there when Pharaoh put him in charge. And God was there when Joseph's family reunited. God worked through Joseph's life *and* his career for His purpose. Joseph chose to be a willing instrument for God's plan and God's glory, just as Proverb 19:21 at the beginning of this section suggests.

> *But Joseph said to them, "Don't be afraid. Am I in the place of God? You intended to harm me, but God intended it for good to accomplish what is now being done, the saving of many lives"* (Genesis 50:19, 20).

Upon the death of their father Israel, the older brothers began to worry about the past abuse and mistreatment they had cast upon Joseph, likely not having ever truly come to peace with their misgivings nor having trusted Joseph's earlier granted forgiveness. In their insecurity, despite the decades gone by, the incidents in which their sinful hatred had expressed itself were still at the forefront of their minds. But Joseph once again kindly reassured his brothers, reminding us how important it is to press forward with God's purpose in our lives. Like the brothers, we can sometimes be tempted to dwell in past misgivings and even be saddled by them. Joseph's ability to be at peace with his past and understand and trust that the Almighty God had a purpose in each of his days is why his journey is such an excellent example for us today.

Chapter Eight

THE LION AND THE GAZELLE

Architecture starts when you carefully put two bricks together. There it begins.
—Ludwig Mies van der Rohe[15]

In chapter three, we wrote about a retail center near our home on which construction had just been started. The work on the building coincided with the writing of this book, and as we complete the writing of this final chapter, work on the structure has just been finished as well. The building is a nicely decorated one-story clad in earth tone materials that will house five businesses. Stone and brick adorn the facade with several black-framed windows across the front. The flat roof mirrors the flat ground below, leveled at the beginning of the building process. Of course, the foundation isn't seen, but it seems to be holding the building in place just fine.

Construction started about a year ago on land that was once the last remnant of a large farm. From the beginning, men and women worked alongside each other to assemble the building piece by piece, and they didn't stop until it was complete. After making the foundation, underground piping was laid for water lines, sewers, and electric wires. The concrete slab was poured, and this later became an interior finished floor. The installation of the roof and the exterior walls followed the erection of the steel framing. The windows and doors were then installed to enclose the structure. The installed electric wires connected to the electrical outlets and lighting, and the heating and air conditioning mechanisms also were attached. Interior walls and exterior brick and stone were put in place as the project neared completion. Final details rounded out the project: parking lot, traffic lights, exterior lighting, handrails, and shrubs. The completed interior touches finished the work. From the installation of the first brick to the last touch, it seemed there was always something that needed to be done to move the project forward.

The quote above from van der Rohe is a fitting start to the last chapter of *Launch Your Life*. There is always a first brick when erecting a building. Even the greatest of museums, longest of bridges, or tallest of buildings were started with the first brick. Then another brick was put on the first brick, another after that, and another after that. Step by step, piece by piece, the materials are assembled to create a more magnificent project. The idea of stacking those first two bricks together lends a clear visual to the concept of the initial effort that applies to you as you build your career in early adult life. Life is built brick by brick. You build some, then you regroup, self-assess, and make changes, but you always strive to make forward progress.

What happens if you give up building midway or decide not to push through to completion for one reason or another? What happens if you get tired or frustrated and decide to stop engaging in bricklaying? Imagine our small retail center with just a handful of bricks, or picture the 1,250-foot Empire State Building having only been started, with bricks stacked only to your waist. While the initial effort is crucial for launch, your continuous determination will carry you forward and set you apart.

Although its origin is unclear, an African proverb inspires us to take this daily approach.

> *Every morning in Africa, a gazelle wakes up. It knows it must run faster than the fastest lion or it will be killed.*

> *Every morning in Africa, a lion wakes up. It knows it must outrun the slowest gazelle or it will starve to death.*
>
> *It doesn't matter whether you are a lion or a gazelle: when the sun comes up, you'd better be running.*

Even if you have never set foot in Africa, the picture is clear, the message is poignant. The lesson regarding your career, your faith, and your life is to keep moving forward each day. As you do, you will continue to grow.

You may have a list of things you would like to improve or change as a result of reading this book, and you may be overwhelmed a bit. It's quite understandable! We suggest you start with one area or one specific attribute. Reflect back to the Preface of this book and the acronym *I-P-A*. Intention, planning, and action. Incorporate *I-P-A* into your thoughts moving forward in that one area. As you develop your dreams and your goals, God will work with you. As you work on implementing your plans, God will work with you. Consider the stories of Peter, David, or any of the many biblical men or women discussed in this book. All continued to lay their individual bricks until something more significant was built. As each of them planned, God helped them grow. When they dreamed, God helped them live. They were the lion. They were the gazelle. And their stories speak to increasing passion and grit as they built their full life and character in service of their God.

Launching your life is about creating your tomorrow. Just as Nehemiah envisioned the reconstructed wall while it was still in piles of rubble, grasp a vision for your future. Think practically about your resume, that one page of paper that puts you in words. Enact a plan in which you can add new lines to it every six months. A new role enhancement on your job, additional responsibilities, or a service project will enrich both your career and your wealth of experience.

Launching your life is about building with the bricks God has given you. Forced from their homes, Daniel, as well as the married couple Priscilla and Aquila, as two examples, set strong examples of career skills and faith. Just as you probably have, they had both good bricks and bad ones, yet their greater life stands as an example for us today. Through life and career, you will continue to receive a variety of bricks you will use to assemble your life. Set your eyes and heart to the greater package of your life by focusing on the path forward. Grasp perseverance, even with the worst of the bricks, and know that God loves you intimately. Keep building.

Launching your life is about growing you and your experience, not about working harder. While there will be times when your work will be demanding and may require extended hours, developing yourself is the more significant point and provides the bigger payoff. Like so many in Lydia's time, as well as today, Lydia had long hours of work from time to time. It was her growth toward an open heart and deep understanding of God, however, that sets her apart for us today. The rounding of her life story and God's use of her and her career is what inspires us, not the extra hours worked. Grow today, tomorrow, and continually in your faith and career and it will surely show in your life.

> *Within your temple, O God, we meditate on your unfailing love. Like your name, O God, your praise reaches to the ends of the earth; your right hand is filled with righteousness. Mount Zion rejoices, the villages of Judah are glad because of your judgments. Walk about Zion, go around her, count her towers, consider well her ramparts, view her citadels, that you may tell of them to the next generation. For this God is our God for ever and ever; he will be our guide even to the end* (Psalm 48:9-14).

The writer of Psalm 48 had his eyes and heart open; he knew his place in creation as well as in God's story. This song starts with the proper exaltation: "Great is the Lord, and most worthy of praise" (48:1). These words anchor the heart and soul of the reader. Like so many psalms, it helps to shift our hearts away from today's activities that can so easily consume us, and it takes us back to the bigger picture of God and the calling to better grasp the work He provides for our journey.

The author goes further than just praise in this psalm, however. The writer seems to be well along in years, as if speaking from personal experience. As we read above, it is more than a direction to sit and ponder God's glory, although that can be helpful. The writer uses the action verbs "walk," "go," "count," "consider," "view," and "tell" in ways that echo the heart and life of the impressive Proverbs 31 Woman. It is a call to exert physical energy toward seeing and understanding God. This expended energy will secure your beliefs and pay your faith forward in ways that will naturally inspire those who follow in your footsteps.

Don't dream, plan, and live without God. Others around you will do so, and some will seem to have great success. But don't be fooled. Besides letting God work through your life and career during your time on earth, both your goal and God's goal is for you to spend eternity with Him. Until then, the Psalm 48 writer gives us a great promise. After several direct words of praise, even calling God the Great King (v. 2), the writer rests his final comforting thoughts on the eternal existence of the creator and the unfailing engagement of God in our lives. Although written well after the time of Joseph, it seems the once-despised teenager could have written these very same words.

For us, the promise is the same. Ever present in our lives, God will escort those who walk forward on the path, His path. Each step forward represents experiences that can produce a new view of God. And while the short view may either encourage or discourage, keep your eyes on the long path ahead and *always find a way to move forward.* Toward the end of your long journey, you will have a magnificent story to tell.

Bibliography

Appalachian Trail Conservancy. "Interactive Map, Thru-Hiking, History." Accessed September 1, 2018. https://appalachiantrail.org/.

Berger, Rob. Forbes Staff. "Top 100 Money Quotes of All Time." April 30, 2014. Accessed October 10, 2018. https://Forbes.com/.

Brainy Quotes. "Ludwig Mies van der Rohe Quotes." Accessed December 4, 2018. https://brainyquotes.com/.

Bryson, Bill. *A Short History of Nearly Everything*. New York: Broadway Books, 2003.

Bryson, Bill. *A Walk in the Woods*. New York: Broadway Books, 1998.

Comey, Joan and Ronald Brownrigg. *Who's Who in the Bible: The Old Testament and The Apocrypha, The New Testament.* New York: Bonanza Books, 1980.

Crouch, Tom D. *The Bishop's Boys.* New York: W. W. Norton & Company, 1989.

Evans, Harold with Gail Buckland and David Lefer. "Wilbur and Orville Wright" and "Henry Ford." In *They Made America*. New York: Little, Brown and Company, 2004.

Fradin, Dennis Brindell. *The Signers: The 56 Stories Behind the Declaration of Independence.* New York: Walker & Company, 2001.

Goalcast. "The 20 Pablo Picasso Quotes to Inspire the Artist in You." Accessed January 24, 2019. https://www.goalcast.com/.

Goodwin, Doris Kearns. *Leadership in Turbulent Times.* New York: Simon & Schuster, Inc., 2018. Kindle.

Limbaugh III, Rush. "My Father's Speech: The Americans Who Risked Everything." Last modified November 21, 2018. https://www.rushlimbaugh.com/daily/2018/11/21/my-fathers-speech-the-americans-who-risked-everything/.

Logue, Victoria and Frank. *The Appalachian Trail Backpacker's Planning Guide.* Birmingham: Menasha Ridge Press, 1991.

McCullough, David. *The Wright Brothers.* New York: Simon & Schuster, Inc., 2015.

Old, Wendie C. *The Wright Brothers: Inventors of the Airplane.* Berkeley Heights: Enslow Publishers, Inc., 2000.

Ong, Desmond. "Famous People Who Have Benefited from Mentors." Accessed August 18, 2018. https.//desmondong.org/.

Packer, J.I. and Merrill C. Tenney and William White, Jr. *Nelson's Illustrated Encyclopedia of Bible Facts.* Nashville: Thomas Nelson Publishers, 1995.

Peters, Tom. "The Brand Called You." *Fast Company.* September 1997.

"The Real Story of New Coke." November 14, 2012. https://www.coca-colacompany.com/stories/coke-lore-new-coke .

Wanderlust Worker. "The Best Way to Predict the Future Is to Create It." Accessed September 15, 2018. https://www.wanderlustworker.com/

Notes

1. Goalcast, "The 20 Pablo Picasso Quotes to Inspire the Artist in You."
2. McCullough, *The Wright Brothers,* pp. 37-39.
3. McCullough, p 217.
4. Bryson, *A Short History of Nearly Everything*, p. 371.
5. Evans, Buckland, Lefer, *They Made America*, p. 239.
6. Evans, Buckland, Lefer, p. 244.
7. Coca-Cola Company, "The Real Story of the New Coke."
8. Limbaugh, "My Father's Speech: The Americans Who Risked Everything."
9. Ong, "Famous People Who Have Benefited from Mentors."
10. Wanderlust Worker, "The Best Way to Predict the Future Is to Create It."
11. Goodwin, *Leadership in Turbulent Times*, Kindle version.
12. Berger, Forbes Staff, "Top 100 Money Quotes of All Time."
13. Appalachian Trail Conservancy, "Thru-Hiking, History."
14. Ibid.
15. Brainy Quotes, Ludwig Mies van der Rohe Quotes.

About the Authors

Philip and Elizabeth Bruns are Christians in the Cincinnati, Ohio area and have led several groups of singles and parents for more than thirty years. They are founders of Launch Ministry (www.launchmini.com), have designed and facilitated multiple workshops, and travel the country speaking to young parents, parents of teenagers, and single professional groups.

Phil and Beth have several mentoring relationships established with both married and single professionals to coach resume writing, including the self-assessment work required to have a great resume and interview. They also help in job search, networking, and career navigation. They focus on times of transition, and their classes emphasize the full life, including faith, marriage, family, career, and academics, all in service of God. As an extension on the idea of transition, they also work with new parents and parents of teens to teach parenting with purpose. Their work helps with building child and teen character, faith, identity, and the family journey for the long haul. They use both biblical and modern-day stories as examples for inspiration.

Professionally, Phil has extensive domestic travel experience and has had successful careers in real estate and construction, holding contractor licenses in five states and serving multiple Fortune 500 clients. Beth has extensive foreign travel experience and has a successful career as an Engineering Research Fellow working in the area of research and development.

They have four faithful adult daughters who have launched or are launching their careers.

For More Information and Resources

You are invited to contact Launch Ministry
www.launchmini.com or email them at hello@launchmini.com
You are also invited to follow them at Launchmini on Facebook,
Instagram, YouTube, and on Twitter.